Barbara Wharram

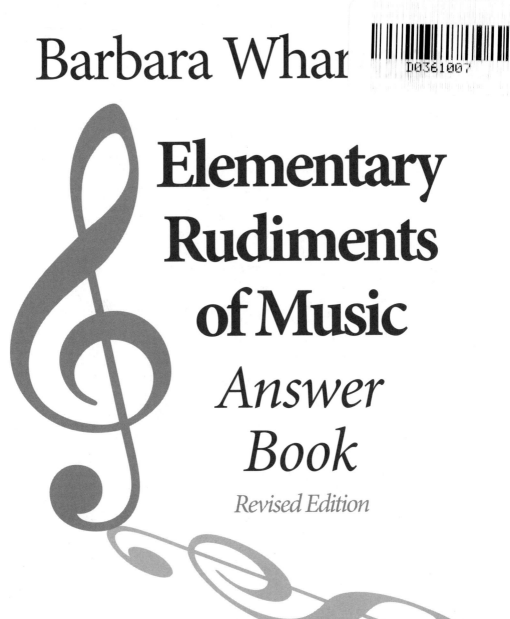

Elementary Rudiments of Music
Answer Book
Revised Edition

Library and Archives Canada Cataloguing in Publication

Answer book, Barbara Wharram, Elementary rudiments of music.

ISBN 1-55440-012-0

1. Music theory--Elementary works--Problems, exercises, etc.

MT7.W55 2005 Suppl.   781   C2005-903191-3

FREDERICK
HARRIS
MUSIC

ISBN-10: 1-55440-012-0
ISBN-13: 978-1-55440-012-6

2

CHAPTER 1

NOTATION

P 1 2 **EXERCISES** (p. 7)

1. Write the following notes in the treble clef.

a) F on a line   f) F in a space
b) A in a space   g) B on a line
c) G on a line   h) D in a space
d) C in a space   i) G in a space
e) E on a line   j) middle C

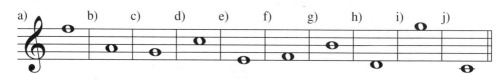

2. Write the following notes in the bass clef.

a) B in a space   f) D on a line
b) F on a line   g) G in a space
c) middle C   h) F in a space
d) A on a line   i) G on a line
e) E in a space   j) C in a space

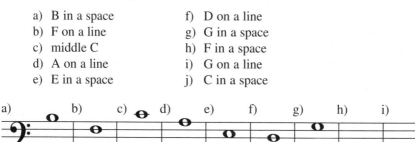

3. Name each of the following notes.

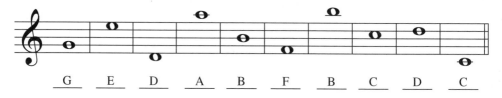

G   E   D   A   B   F   B   C   D   C

4. Name each of the following notes.

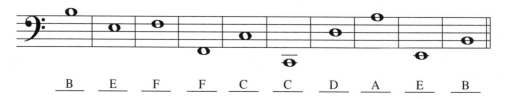

B   E   F   F   C   C   D   A   E   B

5. Name each of the following notes.

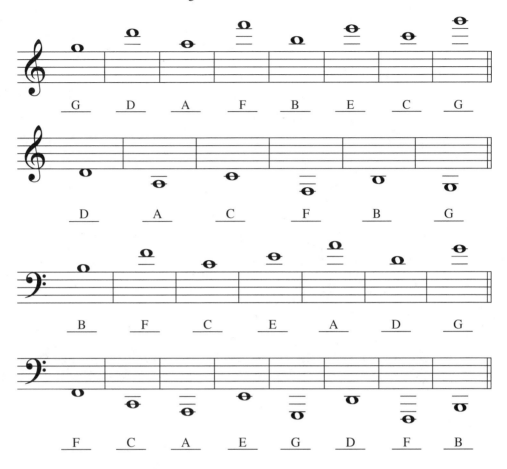

G   D   A   F   B   E   C   G

D   A   C   F   B   G

B   F   C   E   A   D   G

F   C   A   E   G   D   F   B

2   MORE EXERCISES (p. 8)

1. Name each of the following notes.

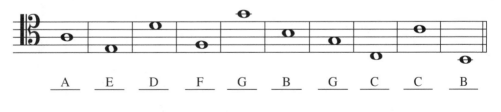

A   E   D   F   G   B   G   C   C   B

2. Name each of the following notes.

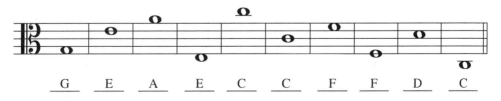

G   E   A   E   C   C   F   F   D   C

3.   Write the following notes in the alto clef.

a) A on a line
b) G on a line
c) D in a space
d) F on a line
e) E in a space

f) B in a space
g) A in a space
h) middle C
i) G in a space
j) E on a line

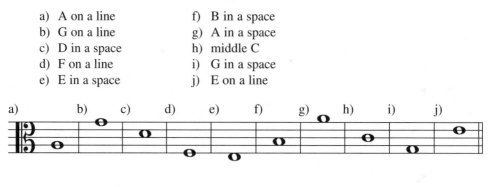

4.   Write the following notes in the tenor clef.

a) D on a line
b) G in a space
c) A on a line
d) E in a space
e) D in a space

f) F on a line
g) middle C
h) F in a space
i) B in a space
j) E on a line

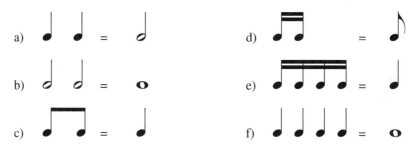

P 1 2   EXERCISES (p. 12)

1.   Write *one* note that is equal to the value of each of the following.

2.   Write *one* rest that is equal to the value of each of the following.

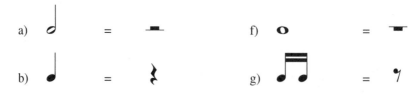

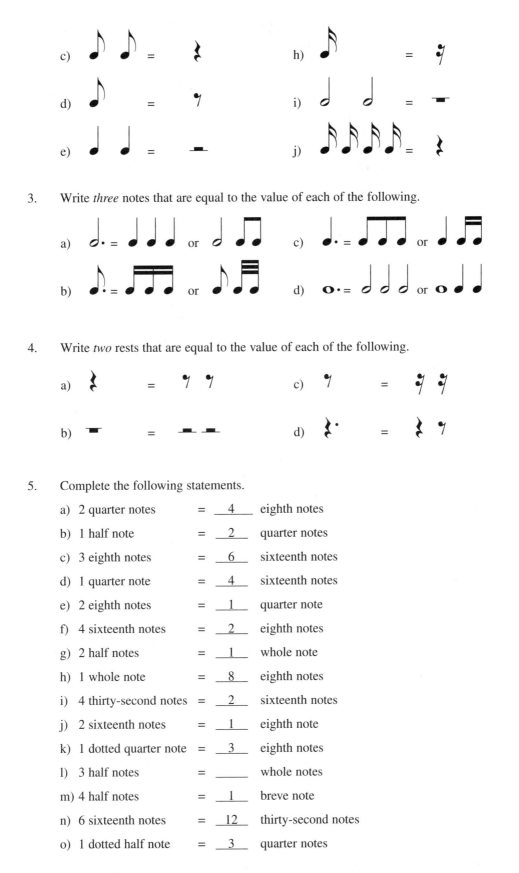

c) ♪ ♪ = 𝄽

h) ♪ = 𝄾

d) ♪ = 𝄾

i) 𝅗𝅥 𝅗𝅥 = 𝄻

e) 𝅘𝅥 𝅘𝅥 = 𝄼

j) ♬♬ = 𝄽

3. Write *three* notes that are equal to the value of each of the following.

a) 𝅗𝅥• = 𝅘𝅥 𝅘𝅥 𝅘𝅥   or 𝅗𝅥 𝅘𝅥 𝅘𝅥

c) 𝅘𝅥• = 𝅘𝅥 𝅘𝅥 𝅘𝅥   or 𝅘𝅥 𝅘𝅥 𝅘𝅥

b) ♪• = ♪ ♪ ♪   or ♪ ♪ ♪

d) 𝅝• = 𝅗𝅥 𝅗𝅥 𝅗𝅥   or 𝅝 𝅘𝅥 𝅘𝅥

4. Write *two* rests that are equal to the value of each of the following.

a) 𝄽 = 𝄾 𝄾

c) 𝄾 = 𝄿 𝄿

b) 𝄻 = 𝄼 𝄼

d) 𝄽• = 𝄽 𝄾

5. Complete the following statements.

a) 2 quarter notes   = _4_ eighth notes

b) 1 half note   = _2_ quarter notes

c) 3 eighth notes   = _6_ sixteenth notes

d) 1 quarter note   = _4_ sixteenth notes

e) 2 eighth notes   = _1_ quarter note

f) 4 sixteenth notes   = _2_ eighth notes

g) 2 half notes   = _1_ whole note

h) 1 whole note   = _8_ eighth notes

i) 4 thirty-second notes   = _2_ sixteenth notes

j) 2 sixteenth notes   = _1_ eighth note

k) 1 dotted quarter note   = _3_ eighth notes

l) 3 half notes   = _____ whole notes

m) 4 half notes   = _1_ breve note

n) 6 sixteenth notes   = _12_ thirty-second notes

o) 1 dotted half note   = _3_ quarter notes

6

6. Write a single note (or a dotted note) that is equal to the value of each of the following.

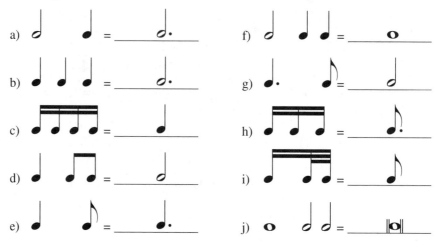

7. Write a single rest (or dotted rest) that is equal to the value of each of the following.

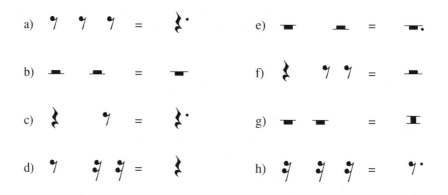

8. Write a single note (or dotted note) that is equal to the value of each of the following.

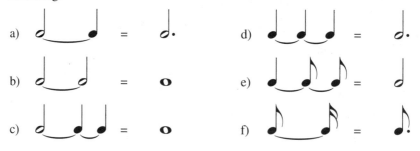

P 1 2   EXERCISES (p. 16)

1. State whether each of the following is a diatonic semitone, a chromatic semitone, or a whole tone.

DS   WT   DS   CS   WT   CS   WT   WT

2. Write a chromatic semitone above each of the following notes.

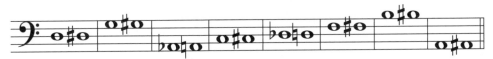

3. Write a diatonic semitone above each of the following notes.

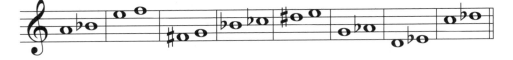

4. Write a chromatic semitone below each of the following notes.

5. Write a diatonic semitone below each of the following notes.

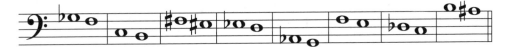

6. Give another name for each of the following notes.

a) F♯ _Gb_ b) Bb _A♯_ c) C _B♯_ d) Ab _G♯_ e) F _E♯_ f) D♯ _Eb_ g) Db _C♯_

7. Name all the whole tones found between pairs of white keys on the piano.

   _C–D, D–E, F–G, G–A, A–B_

8. Name all the whole tones found between pairs of black keys on the piano.

   _C♯–D♯, F♯–G♯, G♯–A♯ or Db–Eb, Gb–Ab, Ab–Bb_

8

8

9. Write a whole tone above each of the following notes.

10. Write a whole tone below each of the following notes.

1 2 **MORE EXERCISES** (p. 17)

1. Complete the following statements.

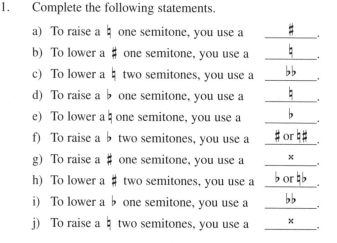

a) To raise a ♮ one semitone, you use a ___♯___.

b) To lower a ♯ one semitone, you use a ___♮___.

c) To lower a ♮ two semitones, you use a ___♭♭___.

d) To raise a ♭ one semitone, you use a ___♮___.

e) To lower a ♮ one semitone, you use a ___♭___.

f) To raise a ♭ two semitones, you use a ___♯ or ♮♯___.

g) To raise a ♯ one semitone, you use a ___×___.

h) To lower a ♯ two semitones, you use a ___♭ or ♮♭___.

i) To lower a ♭ one semitone, you use a ___♭♭___.

j) To raise a ♮ two semitones, you use a ___×___.

2. Write a chromatic semitone above each of the following notes.

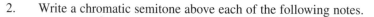

3. Write a chromatic semitone below each of the following notes.

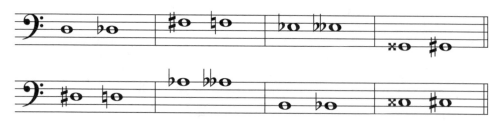

CHAPTER 2

MAJOR AND MINOR SCALES

P 1 2   EXERCISES (p. 22)

1.   Write the following scales in the treble clef, ascending only, using accidentals instead of a key signature. Mark each semitone with a slur, and label the tonic, subdominant, and dominant notes.

a)   A major in half notes

b)   G major in dotted quarter notes

c)   F major in pairs of eighth notes

d)   E♭ major in whole notes

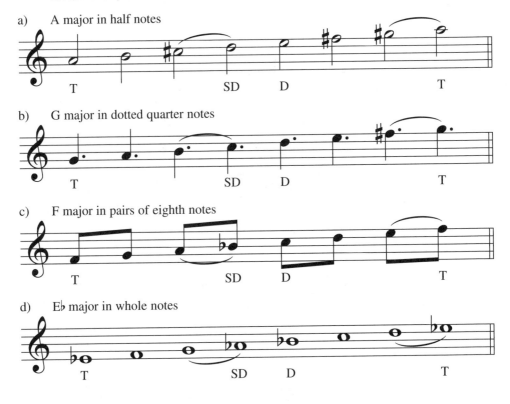

2.   Write the following scales in the bass clef, ascending only, using the correct key signature for each. Mark each semitone with a slur, and label the tonic, subdominant, and dominant notes.

a)   D major in dotted half notes

b)   B♭ major in whole notes

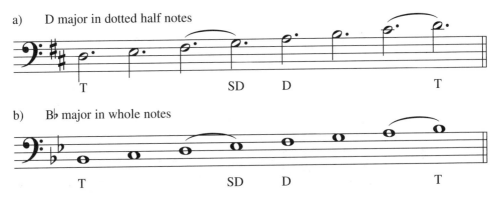

c) E major in quarter notes

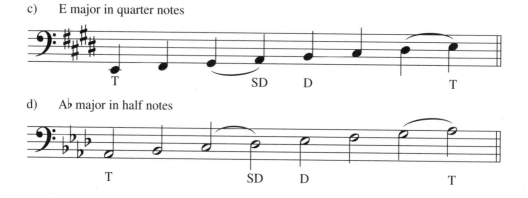

T   SD   D   T

d) A♭ major in half notes

T   SD   D   T

3. Write the following scales in the treble clef, ascending and descending, using accidentals instead of a key signature. Mark each semitone with a slur, and label the tonic, subdominant, and dominant notes.

a) E major in whole notes

T   SD   D   T   D   SD   T

b) A♭ major in dotted half notes

T   SD   D   T   D   SD   T

c) C major in half notes

T   SD   D   T   D   SD   T

d) B♭ major in pairs of eighth notes

T   SD   D   T   D   SD   T

e) D major in quarter notes

T   SD   D   T   D   SD   T

4. Write the following scales in the bass clef, ascending and descending, using the correct key signature for each. Mark each semitone with a slur, and label the tonic, subdominant, and dominant notes.

a) Eb major in half notes

b) G major in pairs of eighth notes

c) F major in dotted quarter notes

d) A major in whole notes

5. Write the following key signatures in the treble clef.

    a) Ab major   c) Bb major
    b) E major   d) D major

6. Write the following key signatures in the bass clef.

    a) F major   c) Eb major
    b) A major   d) G major

12

7. Write the following notes in the treble clef, using the correct key signature for each.

a) the tonic of F major
b) the tonic of E♭ major
c) the dominant of D major
d) the subdominant of B♭ major

e) the dominant of A major
f) the dominant of G major
g) the tonic of A♭ major
h) the subdominant of E major

8. Write the following notes in the bass clef, using the correct key signature for each.

a) the tonic of E major
b) the dominant of B♭ major
c) the subdominant of F major
d) the subdominant of D major

e) the dominant of A♭ major
f) the tonic of C major
g) the subdominant of G major
h) the dominant of E♭ major

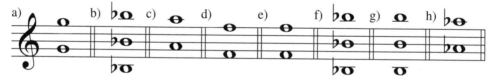

9. Write the following notes in the treble clef, using accidentals instead of key signatures.

a) the tonic of G major
b) the subdominant of F major
c) the dominant of D major
d) the dominant of B♭ major

e) the subdominant of C major
f) the tonic of B♭ major
g) the dominant of E major
h) the subdominant of E♭ major

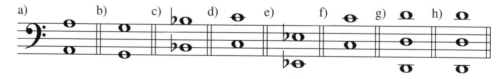

10. Write the following notes in the bass clef, using accidentals instead of key signatures.

a) the tonic of A major
b) the dominant of C major
c) the dominant of E♭ major
d) the subdominant of G major

e) the subdominant of B♭ major
f) the dominant of F major
g) the subdominant of A major
h) the tonic of D major

11. Fill in the blanks in the following sentences.

a) The key signature of D major is 2 sharps   F♯, C♯.

b) The tonic of E♭ major is _____ E♭ _____.

c) The key signature of A♭ major is 4 flats   B♭, E♭, A♭, D♭ .

d) The major key that has three sharps is ____ A major ____.

e) [musical notation] is the key signature of ____ G ____ major.

f) The major key that has two flats is ___ B♭ major ___.

g) The order of the first four sharps is F♯, C♯, G♯, D♯ .

h) Semitones occur between 3rd and 4th, and 7th and 8th in every major scale.

i) The dominant of C major is ____ G ____.

j) The names of the flats in E♭ major are B♭, E♭, A♭ .

k) The key signature of E major is 4 sharps   F♯, C♯, G♯, D♯ .

l) D is the subdominant of A major.

m) The major key that has four flats is ___ A♭ major ___.

n) The fifth note of any scale is called the dominant .

o) A scale can be divided into two tetrachords .

p) F is the dominant of ____ B♭ ____ major.

q) [musical notation] is the key signature of ____ F ____ major.

r) The order of tones and semitones in every major scale is T, T, ST, T, T, T, ST .

s) E♭ is the subdominant of ____ B♭ ____ major.

t) The key that has no sharps or flats is ____ C ____ major.

1 2   MORE EXERCISES (p. 26)

1. Write the following notes in the treble clef, using the correct key signature for each.

a) the mediant of B major
b) the dominant of F♯ major
c) the tonic of G♭ major
d) the submediant of D major
e) the supertonic of A major

f) the leading note of E♭ major
g) the subdominant of C♯ major
h) the dominant of A♭ major
i) the supertonic of B♭ major
j) the leading note of E major

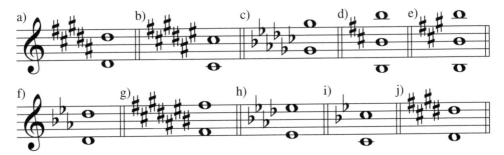

2. Write the following notes in the bass clef, using the correct key signature for each.

a) the tonic of D♭ major
b) the submediant of F major
c) the supertonic of C major
d) the dominant of E♭ major
e) the leading note of G major

f) the mediant of F♯ major
g) the subdominant of A major
h) the submediant of A♭ major
i) the mediant of B♭ major
j) the tonic of B major

3. Write the following notes in the treble clef, using accidentals instead of a key signature.

a) the subdominant of C major
b) the tonic of E♭ major
c) the dominant of D major
d) the mediant of A major

e) the submediant of G major
f) the dominant of B major
g) the supertonic of A♭ major
h) the leading note of C♯ major

4. Write the following notes in the bass clef, using accidentals instead of a key signature.

a) the leading note of A major
b) the supertonic of G♭ major
c) the dominant of E major
d) the submediant of B♭ major

e) the mediant of C♯ major
f) the leading note of B major
g) the supertonic of D major
h) the subdominant of G major

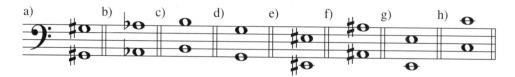

5.   List the order of the sharps as they appear in a key signature.

F♯ C♯ G♯ D♯ A♯ E♯ B♯

6.   List the order of the flats as they appear in a key signature.

B♭ E♭ A♭ D♭ G♭ C♭ F♭

7.   Name the major key and the technical degree name of each of the following.

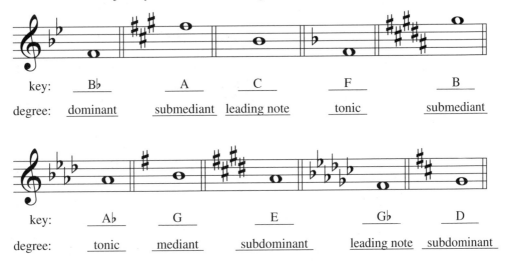

key: B♭   A   C   F   B

degree: dominant   submediant leading note tonic   submediant

key: A♭   G   E   G♭   D

degree: tonic   mediant   subdominant leading note subdominant

8.   Name the major key and the technical degree name of each of the following.

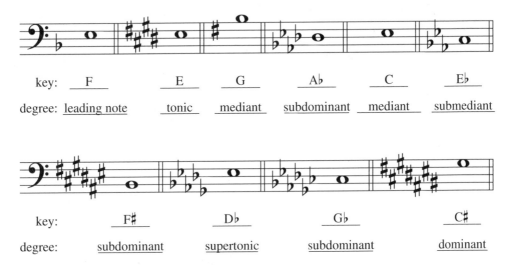

key: F   E   G   A♭   C   E♭

degree: leading note   tonic   mediant   subdominant   mediant   submediant

key: F♯   D♭   G♭   C♯

degree: subdominant   supertonic   subdominant   dominant

9. Write the following scales, ascending and descending, in the treble clef.
    Use accidentals instead of a key signature, and mark the semitones with slurs.

a)   F♯ major in half notes

b)   C♭ major in quarter notes

c)   D♭ major in eighth notes

10. Write the following scales, ascending and descending, in the treble clef. Use the
     correct key signature for each, and mark the semitones with slurs.

a)   C♯ major in sixteenth notes

b)   B major in half notes

c)   G♭ major in whole notes

11. Write the following scales, ascending and descending, in the bass clef. Use accidentals
     instead of a key signature, and mark the semitones with slurs.

a)   B major in quarter notes

17

b)   C♯ major in eighth notes

c)   G♭ major in dotted half notes

12.   Write the following scales, ascending and descending, in the bass clef. Use the correct key signature for each, and mark the semitones with slurs.

a)   F♯ major in dotted quarter notes

b)   D♭ major in whole notes

c)   C♭ major in sixteenth notes

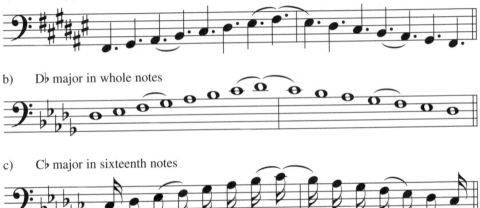

13.   Write the following scales in the treble clef, ascending only. Use the correct key signature for each. Use whole notes.

a) the major scale whose key signature is five flats
b) the major scale whose dominant is G♯
c) the major scale whose leading note is A♯
d) the major scale whose key signature is six flats
e) the major scale whose supertonic is G♯
f) the major scale whose mediant is E♭
g) the major scale whose subdominant is F♯
h) the major scale whose submediant is G♯
i) the major scale whose leading note is F
j) the major scale whose mediant is G

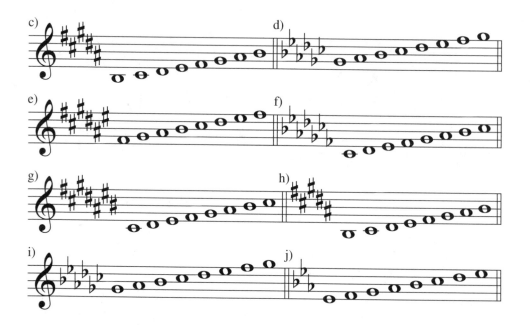

2 STILL MORE EXERCISES (p. 30)

1. Write the following scales in the alto clef, ascending and descending. Use the correct key signature for each, and mark the semitones with slurs. Use whole notes.

a) B♭ major

b) D major

c) G♭ major

d) C♯ major

e) F major

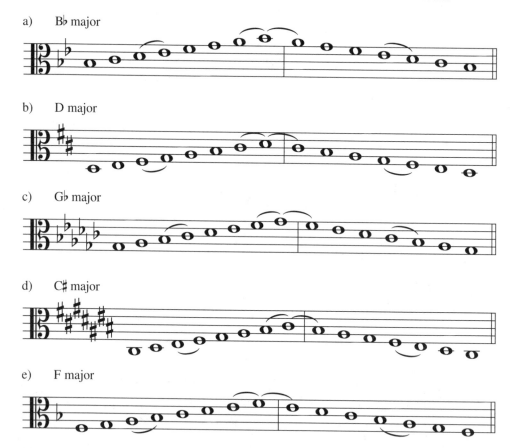

f)   B major

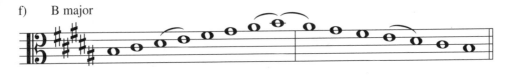

g)   E♭ major

2.   Write the following scales in the alto clef, ascending and descending. Use accidentals instead of a key signature, and mark the semitones with slurs. Use whole notes.

a)   A major

b)   D♭ major

c)   F♯ major

d)   C major

e)   A♭ major

f)   E major

g)   G major

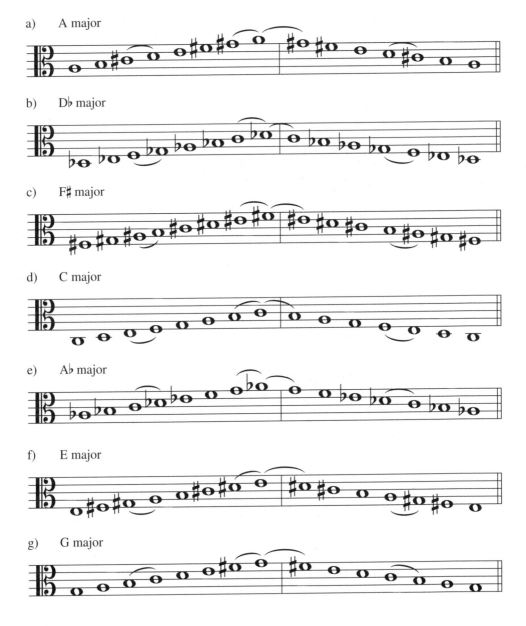

3. Write the following scales in the tenor clef, descending only. Use the correct key signature for each, and mark the semitones with slurs. Use whole notes.

a) C major

b) E major

c) G major

d) A major

e) D♭ major

f) F♯ major

g) A♭ major

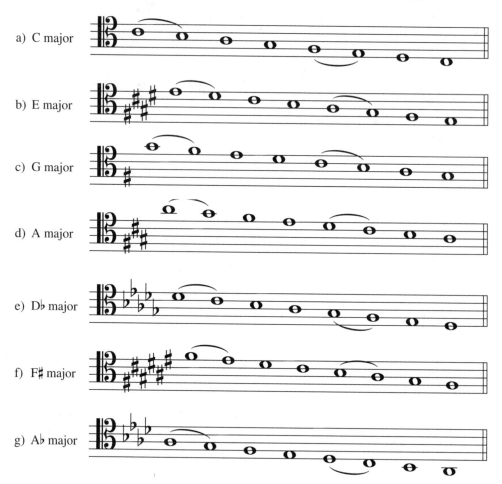

4. Write the following scales in the tenor clef, descending only. Use accidentals instead of a key signature, and mark the semitones with slurs. Use whole notes.

a) C♯ major

b) E♭ major

c) F major

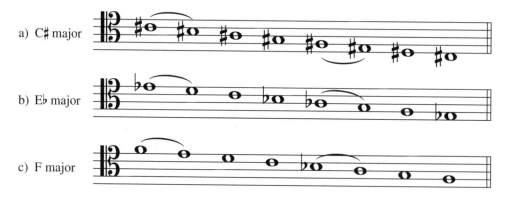

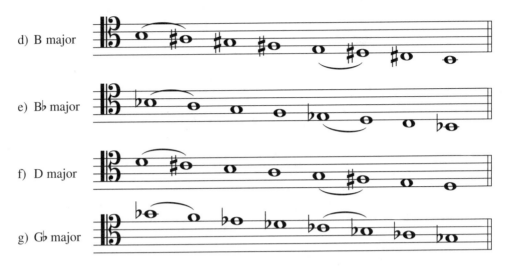

d) B major

e) B♭ major

f) D major

g) G♭ major

5. Write the following scales in the bass clef, ascending and descending. Use the correct key signature, and mark the semitones with slurs. Use whole notes.

a) B♭ major, from dominant to dominant

b) E major, from supertonic to supertonic

c) D♭ major, from subdominant to subdominant

d) G major, from submediant to submediant

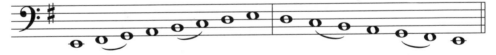

e) C♯ major, from tonic to tonic

6. Write the following scales in the treble clef, ascending and descending. Use accidentals instead of a key signature, and mark the semitones with slurs. Use whole notes.

a) A major, from mediant to mediant

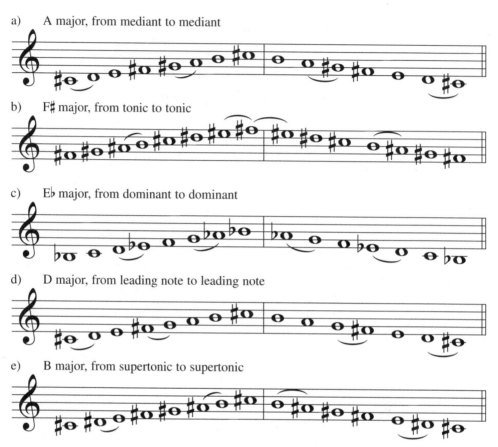

b) F♯ major, from tonic to tonic

c) E♭ major, from dominant to dominant

d) D major, from leading note to leading note

e) B major, from supertonic to supertonic

7. Write the following scales in the alto clef, ascending and descending. Use the correct key signature, and mark the semitones with slurs. Use whole notes.

a) A♭ major, from dominant to dominant

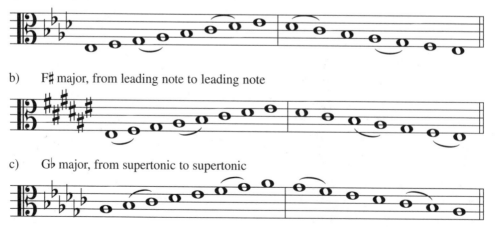

b) F♯ major, from leading note to leading note

c) G♭ major, from supertonic to supertonic

d)   B major, from subdominant to subdominant

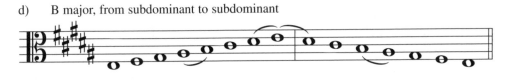

e)   A major, from submediant to submediant

8.   Write the following scales in the tenor clef, ascending and descending. Use accidentals instead of a key signature, and mark the semitones with slurs. Use whole notes.

a)   D♭ major, from tonic to tonic

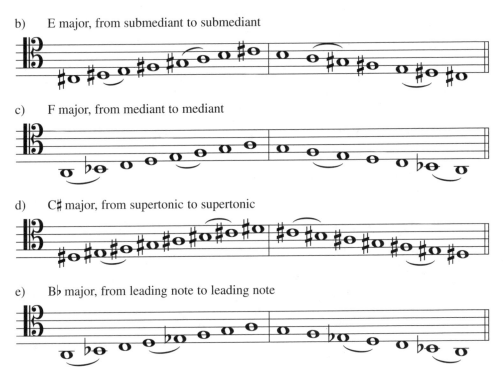

b)   E major, from submediant to submediant

c)   F major, from mediant to mediant

d)   C♯ major, from supertonic to supertonic

e)   B♭ major, from leading note to leading note

24

1. Name the relative major of the following minor keys.

    a) C♯ minor _____   d) B minor_____

    b) A minor _____   e) G minor____B♭ major____

    c) F minor ____A♭ major____   f) E minor_____

2. Name the relative minor of the following major keys.

    a) A major ____F♯ minor____   d) E major ____C♯ minor____

    b) E♭ major _____   e) G major_____

    c) F major _____   f) B♭ major _____

3. Fill in the blanks in the following sentences.

    a) The minor key whose key signature is one sharp is _____.

    b) The key signature of B minor is _____ _F♯, C♯_ .

    c) The key signature of A major is _____ _F♯, C♯, G♯_ .

    d) The major key whose key signature is four flats is _A♭ major_ .

    e) The subdominant of D minor is ____G____ .

    f) The minor key whose key signature is three sharps is _F♯ minor_ .

    g) The key signature of E♭ major is _____ _B♭, E♭, A♭_ .

    h) The dominant of F♯ minor is ____C♯____ .

    i) The major key whose key signature is two flats is _B♭ major_ .

    j) The key signature of F minor is _____ _B♭, E♭, A♭, D♭_ .

    k) The minor key whose key signature is two flats is _____.

    l) The major key whose key signature is one sharp is _____.

    m) The key signature of C♯ minor is _____ _F♯, C♯, G♯, D♯_ .

    n) The dominant of B minor is ____F♯____ .

    o) The key signature of F major is _____ _B♭_ .

    p) The key signature of D minor is _____ _B♭_ .

    q) The major key whose key signature is four sharps is _____.

    r) The minor key whose key signature is three flats is _____.

    s) The key signature of D major is _____ _F♯, C♯_ .

    t) The subdominant of C♯ minor is ____F♯____ .

4. Write the following scales in the treble clef, ascending and descending. Use the correct key signature for each, and mark the semitones with slurs. Use whole notes.

a) E minor, natural form

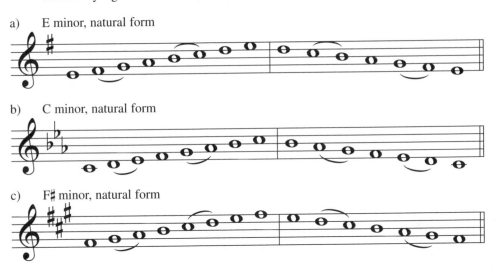

b) C minor, natural form

c) F♯ minor, natural form

5. Write the following scales in the treble clef, ascending and descending. Use the correct key signature for each, and label the tonic, subdominant, and dominant notes. Use whole notes.

a) A minor harmonic

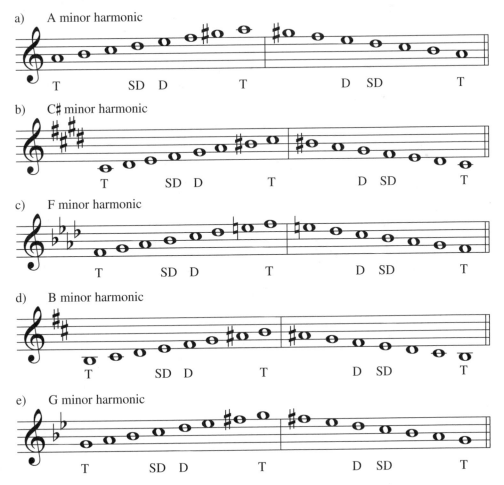

T   SD D   T   D SD   T

b) C♯ minor harmonic

T   SD D   T   D SD   T

c) F minor harmonic

T   SD D   T   D SD   T

d) B minor harmonic

T   SD D   T   D SD   T

e) G minor harmonic

T   SD D   T   D SD   T

6.　Write the following scales in the bass clef, ascending and descending.
Use accidentals instead of a key signature. Use whole notes.

a)　D minor melodic

b)　E minor melodic

c)　C minor melodic

d)　F♯ minor melodic

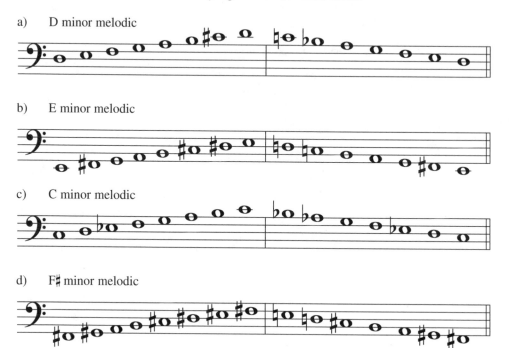

7.　Write the following scales in the treble clef, ascending and descending.
Use accidentals instead of a key signature, and label the tonic, subdominant, and
dominant notes. Use whole notes.

a)　D minor, natural form

b)　B minor, natural form

c)　F minor, natural form

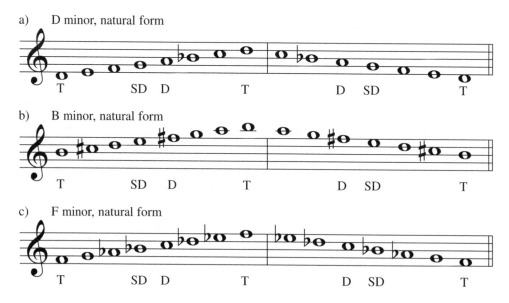

8. Write the following scales in the bass clef, ascending and descending. Use the correct key signature and label the tonic, subdominant, and dominant notes. Use whole notes.

a) C minor harmonic

b) F♯ minor harmonic

c) E minor harmonic

d) D minor harmonic

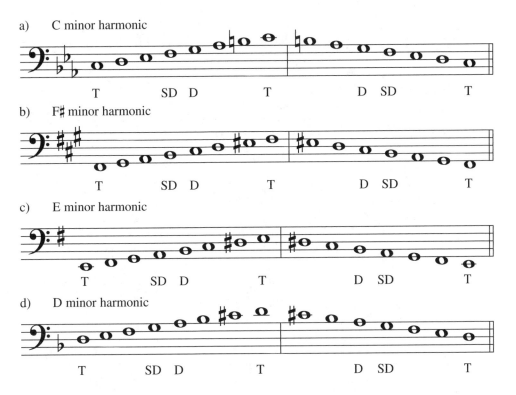

9. Write the following scales in the treble clef, ascending and descending. Use accidentals instead of a key signature. Use whole notes.

a) B minor melodic

b) G minor melodic

c) A minor melodic

d) C♯ minor melodic

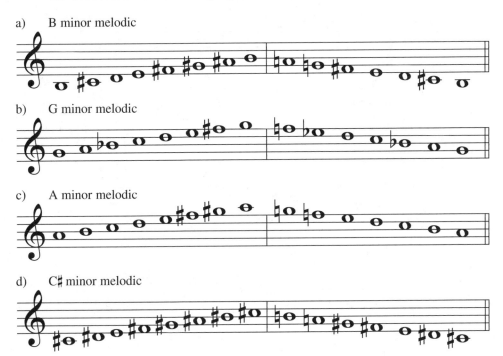

28

10. Write the following scales in the bass clef, ascending and descending. Use the correct key signature for each, and mark the semitones with slurs. Use whole notes.

a)　G minor, natural form

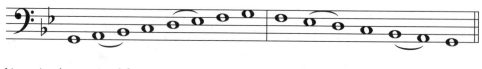

b)　A minor, natural form

c)　C♯ minor, natural form

d)　F minor, natural form

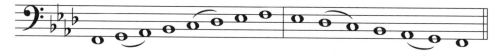

11. Write the following scales in the treble clef, ascending and descending. Use accidentals instead of a key signature, and mark the semitones with slurs. Use whole notes.

a)　E minor harmonic

b)　D minor harmonic

c)　F♯ minor harmonic

d)　C minor harmonic

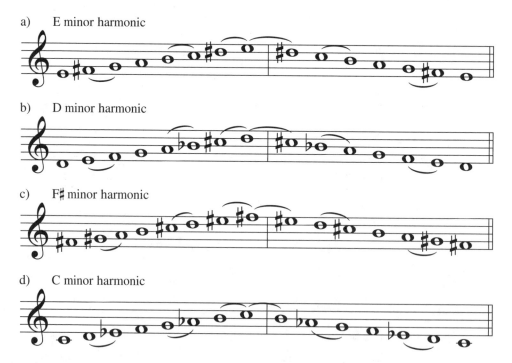

12. Write the following scales in the bass clef, ascending and descending. Use the correct key signature for each, and mark the semitones with slurs. Use whole notes.

a) B minor melodic

b) F minor melodic

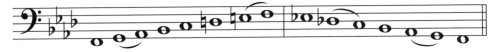

c) C# minor melodic

d) G minor melodic

13. Write the following scales in the bass clef, ascending and descending. Use accidentals instead of a key signature, and mark the semitones with slurs. Use whole notes.

a) C# minor harmonic

b) F minor harmonic

c) A minor harmonic

d) G minor harmonic

14. Write the following scales in the treble clef, ascending and descending. Use the correct key signature for each, and mark the semitones with slurs. Use whole notes.

a) F♯ minor melodic

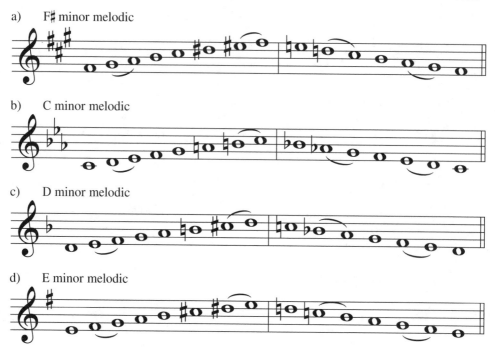

b) C minor melodic

c) D minor melodic

d) E minor melodic

1 2 MORE EXERCISES (p. 49)

1. Write the following scales in the treble clef, ascending and descending. Use the correct key signature for each, and mark the semitones with slurs. Use whole notes.

a) G♯ minor, natural form

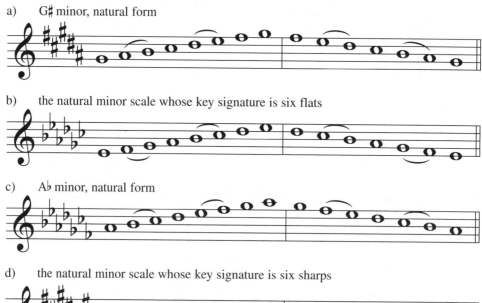

b) the natural minor scale whose key signature is six flats

c) A♭ minor, natural form

d) the natural minor scale whose key signature is six sharps

2.   Write the following scales in the bass clef, ascending and descending. Use accidentals instead of key signatures, and mark the semitones with slurs. Use whole notes.

a)   B♭ minor, natural form

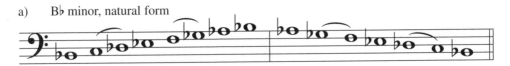

b)   the natural minor scale whose relative major is E

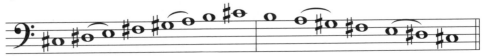

c)   A♯ minor, natural form

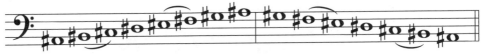

d)   the natural minor scale whose relative major is A♭

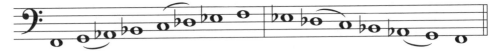

3.   Write the following scales in the treble clef, ascending and descending. Use the correct key signature for each, and mark the semitones with slurs. Use whole notes.

a)   D♯ minor melodic

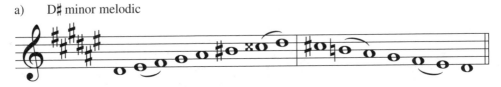

b)   the melodic minor scale whose relative major is D♭

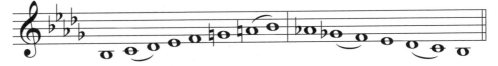

c)   the melodic minor scale whose key signature is seven flats

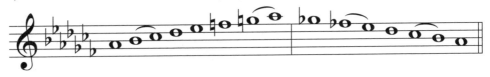

4. Write the following scales in the treble clef, ascending and descending.
    Use accidentals instead of a key signature, and mark the semitones with slurs.
    Use whole notes.

a)   A# minor melodic

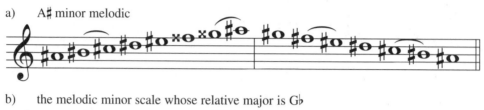

b)   the melodic minor scale whose relative major is G♭

c)   the melodic minor scale whose key signature is five sharps

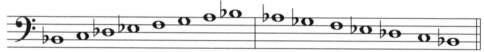

5. Write the following scales in the bass clef, ascending and descending, using
    accidentals instead of a key signature. Use whole notes.

a)   B♭ minor melodic

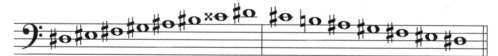

b)   the melodic minor scale whose relative major is F#

c)   the melodic minor scale whose key signature is seven flats

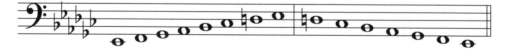

6. Write the following scales in the bass clef, ascending and descending, using the correct
    key signature for each. Use whole notes.

a)   E♭ minor harmonic

b)   the harmonic minor scale whose relative major is B

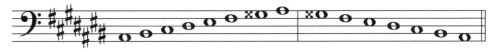

c)   the harmonic minor scale whose key signature is seven sharps

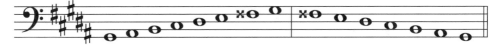

7.   Write the following scales in the treble clef, ascending and descending, using the correct key signature for each. Use whole notes.

a)   A♭ major

its relative minor, harmonic

its tonic minor, melodic

b)   B♭ major

its relative minor, melodic

its tonic minor, harmonic

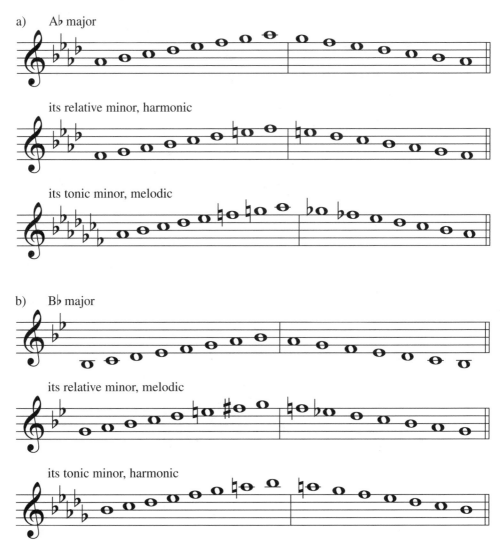

34

c)   F major

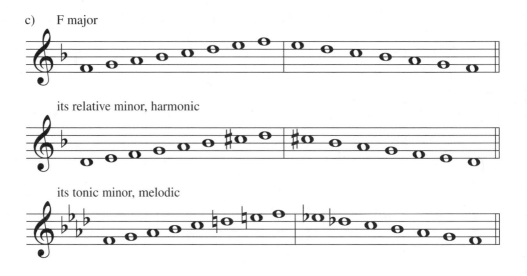

its relative minor, harmonic

its tonic minor, melodic

8.   Write the following scales ascending and descending, in the bass clef, using the correct key signature for each. Use whole notes.

a)   the melodic minor scale whose supertonic is D

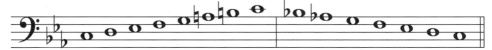

b)   the harmonic minor scale whose dominant is B♭

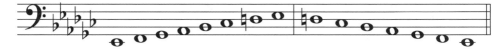

c)   the melodic minor scale whose leading note is G♯

d)   the harmonic minor scale whose subdominant is E♭

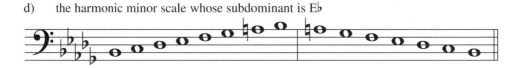

e)   the harmonic minor scale whose mediant is A

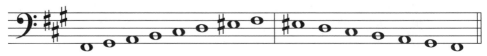

9. Add the proper clef, key signature, and accidentals where necessary, to complete the following scales.

a) G♭ major

b) E major

c) G minor melodic

d) E♭ major

e) E minor harmonic

f) G♯ minor harmonic

2 STILL MORE EXERCISES (p. 54)

1. Write the following scales in the given clefs, ascending and descending. Use the correct key signature for each. Use whole notes.

a) E♭ minor, natural form

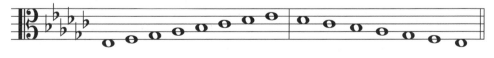

b) C minor, natural form

c)   A♯ minor, natural form

2.   Write the following scales in the given clefs, ascending and descending.
      Use accidentals instead of a key signature. Use whole notes.

a)   F minor, natural form

b)   G minor, natural form

c)   C♯ minor, natural form

3.   Write the following scales in the alto clef, ascending and descending, using the
      correct key signature for each. Use whole notes.

a)   A♭ minor harmonic

b)   B minor melodic

c)   D♯ minor harmonic

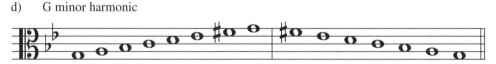

d)   G minor harmonic

4. Write the following scales in the tenor clef, ascending and descending, using the correct key signature for each. Use whole notes.

a) C minor melodic

b) G♯ minor harmonic

c) E minor melodic

d) F♯ minor melodic

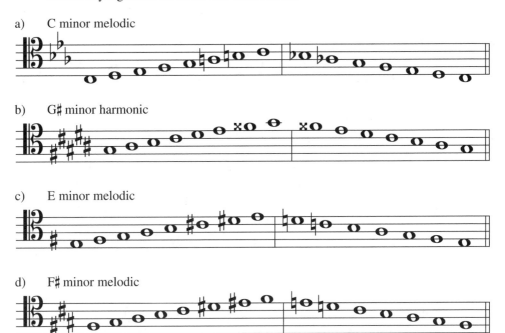

5. Write the following scales in the alto clef, ascending and descending, using accidentals instead of a key signature. Use whole notes.

a) C minor harmonic

b) E minor harmonic

c) D minor melodic

d) F♯ minor harmonic

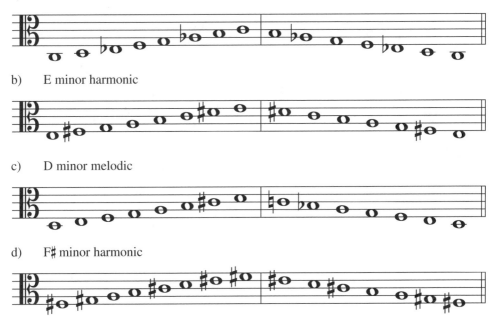

6. Write the following scales in the tenor clef, ascending and descending, using accidentals instead of a key signature. Use whole notes.

a) B minor harmonic

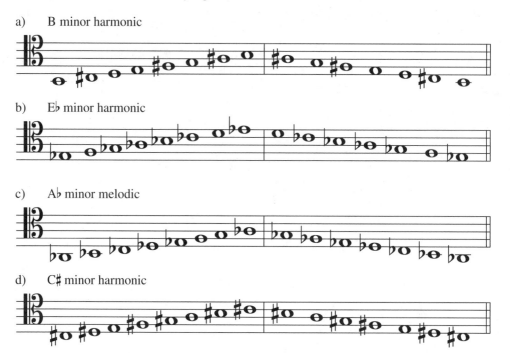

b) E♭ minor harmonic

c) A♭ minor melodic

d) C♯ minor harmonic

7. Write the following scales in the given clefs, ascending and descending. Use the correct key signature for each. Use whole notes.

a) D♯ minor, natural form, from supertonic to supertonic

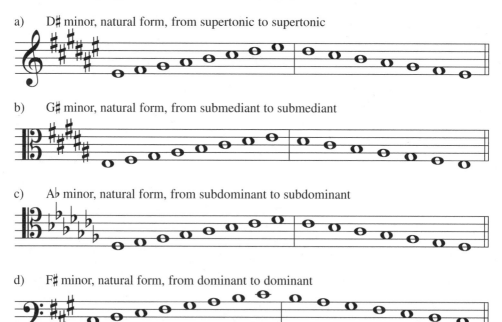

b) G♯ minor, natural form, from submediant to submediant

c) A♭ minor, natural form, from subdominant to subdominant

d) F♯ minor, natural form, from dominant to dominant

e)   B♭ minor, natural form, from mediant to mediant

8.   Write the following scales, ascending and descending, in the bass clef. Use the correct key signature for each, and mark the semitones with slurs. Use whole notes.

a)   G♯ minor melodic, from dominant to dominant

b)   C♯ minor harmonic, from subdominant to subdominant

c)   E minor harmonic, from dominant to dominant

d)   B♭ minor melodic, from tonic to tonic

e)   F♯ minor harmonic, from subdominant to subdominant

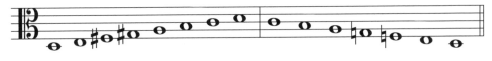

9.   Write the following scales in the alto clef, ascending and descending, using the correct key signature for each. Use whole notes.

a)   A minor melodic, from subdominant to subdominant

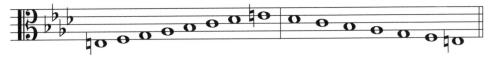

b)   F minor harmonic, from leading note to leading note

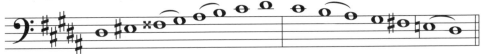

40

c)   G♯ minor harmonic, from mediant to mediant

d)   B minor harmonic, from leading note to leading note

e)   C minor melodic, from supertonic to supertonic

f)   E♭ minor harmonic, from submediant to submediant

g)   D minor harmonic, from dominant to dominant

h)   F♯ minor melodic, from supertonic to supertonic

i)   B♭ minor harmonic, from subdominant to subdominant

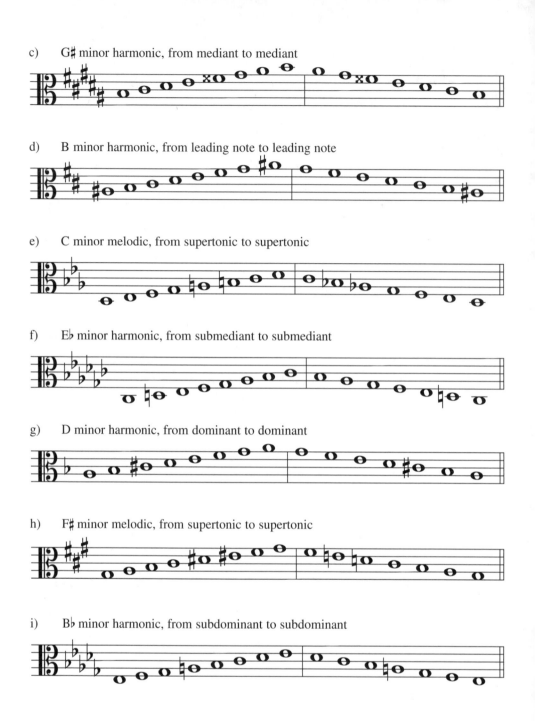

10. Write the following scales in the tenor clef, ascending and descending, using the correct key signature for each. Use whole notes.

a) the major scale whose key signature is six sharps

b) its relative minor, harmonic

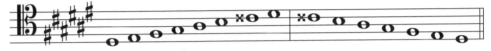

c) its tonic minor, melodic

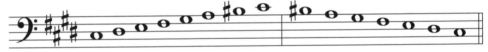

11. Write the following scales in the bass clef, ascending and descending, using the correct key signature for each. Use whole notes.

a) the harmonic minor scale whose key signature is four sharps

b) its relative major

c) its tonic major

12. Add the proper clef, key signature, and accidentals where necessary to complete the following scales.

a)   D major, from mediant to mediant

b)   G minor melodic, from submediant to submediant

c)   C♯ major, from submediant to submediant

d)   F♯ minor harmonic, from tonic to tonic

e)   A minor melodic, from tonic to tonic

f)   E minor melodic, from mediant to mediant

g)   B♭ major, from dominant to dominant

h)   C minor harmonic, from mediant to mediant

i)   F minor harmonic, from supertonic to supertonic

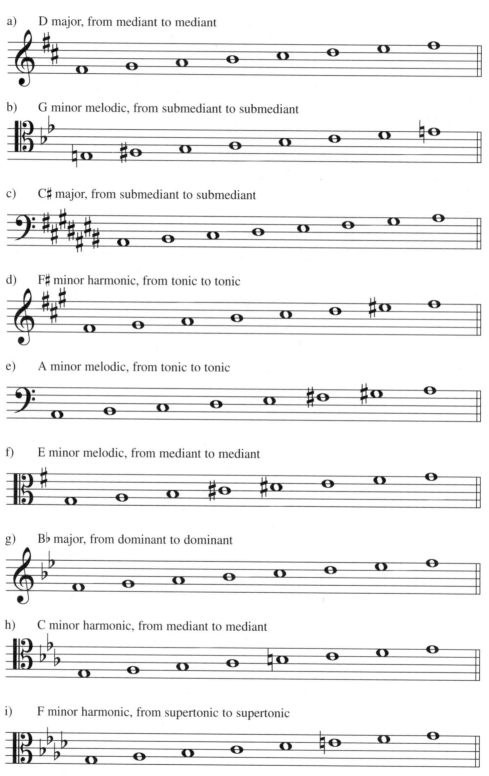

13. Write the following scales in the treble clef, ascending and descending, using the correct key signature for each. Use whole notes.

a) Eb major

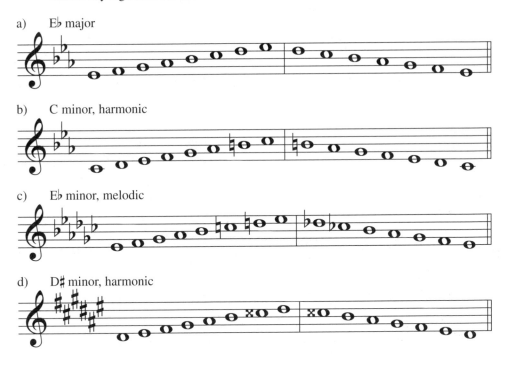

b) C minor, harmonic

c) Eb minor, melodic

d) D# minor, harmonic

State the relationship of the first scale in question 13 to each of the others.

   relationship of a) to b) _a) is relative major of b)_

   relationship of a) to c) _a) is tonic major of c)_

   relationship of a) to d) _a) is enharmonic tonic major of d)_

CHAPTER 3

OTHER SCALES AND MODES

1 2   EXERCISES (p. 64)

1. Write the following scales in the treble clef, ascending and descending, using accidentals. Use whole notes.

a)   chromatic scale starting on G

b)   chromatic scale starting on F

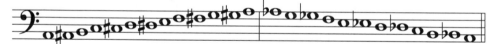

c)   chromatic scale starting on F♯

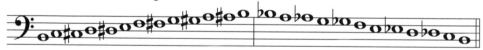

2. Write the following scales in the bass clef, ascending and descending, using accidentals. Use whole notes.

a)   chromatic scale starting on A

b)   chromatic scale starting on B

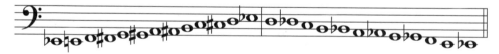

c)   chromatic scale starting on E♭

3. Add accidentals to each of the following to create chromatic scales.

a)

45

b)

c)

d)

4. Write the following scales in the treble clef, ascending and descending, using key signatures. Use whole notes.

a) chromatic scale starting on B♭

b) chromatic scale starting on D

c) chromatic scale starting on B

5. Write the following scales in the bass clef, ascending and descending, using key signatures. Use whole notes.

a) chromatic scale starting on A

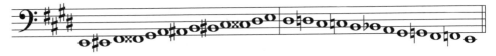

b) chromatic scale starting on E

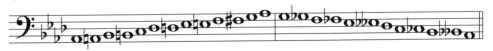

c) chromatic scale starting on A♭

2   MORE EXERCISES (p. 66)

1.   Write the following scales in the given clefs, ascending and descending, using accidentals. Use whole notes.

a)   chromatic scale starting on F♯

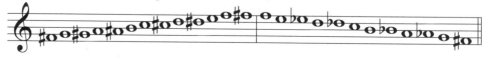

b)   chromatic scale starting on D

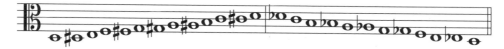

c)   chromatic scale starting on B♭

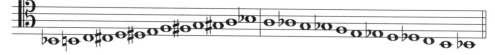

d)   chromatic scale starting on D♭

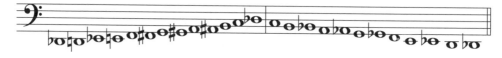

2.   Write the following scales in the given clefs, ascending and descending, using key signatures. Use whole notes.

a)   chromatic scale starting on C♯

b)   chromatic scale starting on A♭

c)   chromatic scale starting on E

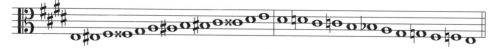

d)   chromatic scale starting on G♭

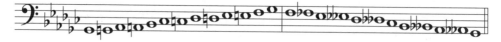

1 2   EXERCISES (p. 68)

1.   Change each of the following major 2nds into a diminished 3rd by respelling one of
its notes enharmonically.

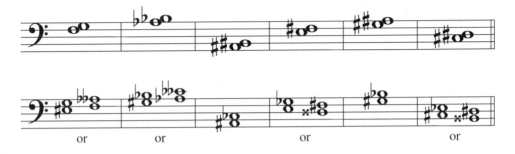

2.   Change each of the following diminished 3rds into a major 2nd by respelling one of
its notes enharmonically.

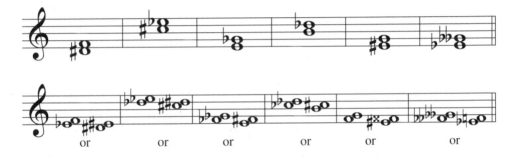

3.   Add accidentals to each of the following to create whole tone scales. Do not alter the
first note of each scale.

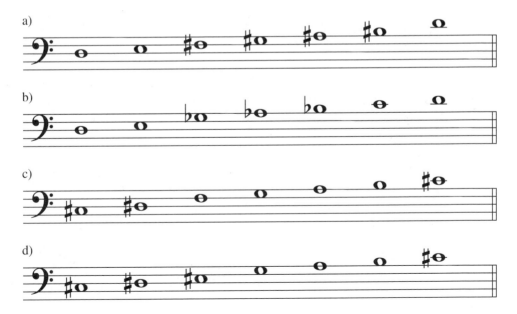

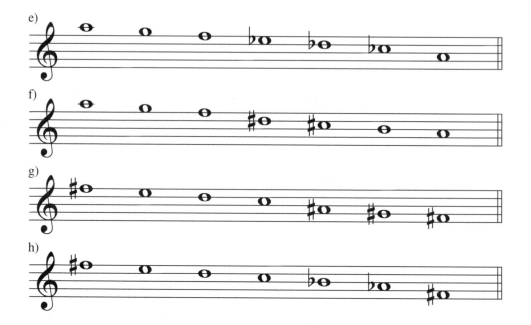

4.   Write a whole tone scale in the treble clef, ascending and descending, beginning on each of the following notes. (Sample answers. Other spellings are possible.)

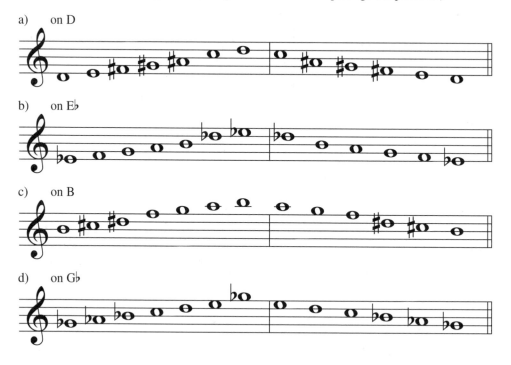

5. Write a whole tone scale in the bass clef, ascending and descending, beginning on each of the following notes. (Sample answers. Other spellings are possible.)

a) on A

b) on E

c) on F♯

d) on C♯

2 MORE EXERCISES (p. 71)

1. Write a whole tone scale in the tenor clef, ascending and descending, beginning on each of the following notes. (Sample answers. Other spellings are possible.)

a) on D♭

b) on F♯

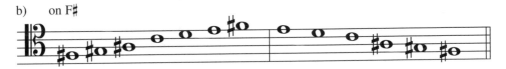

c) on A

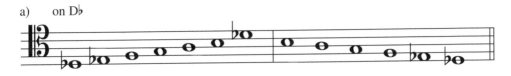

d) on B♭

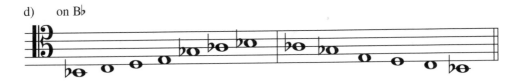

2. Write a whole tone scale in the alto clef, ascending and descending, beginning on each of the following notes. (Sample answers. Other spellings are possible.)

a) on G

b) on Ab

c) on C♯

d) on B

1 2 EXERCISES (p. 72)

1. Add accidentals to each of the following to create blues scales. Do not alter the first note of each scale.

a)

b)

c)

d)

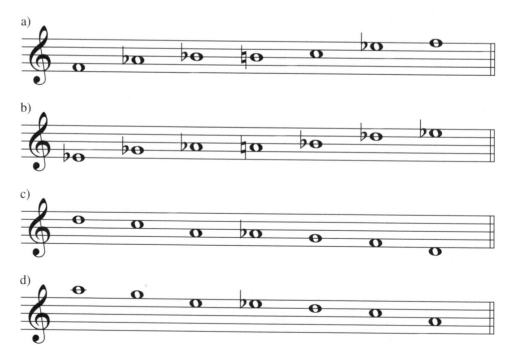

e)

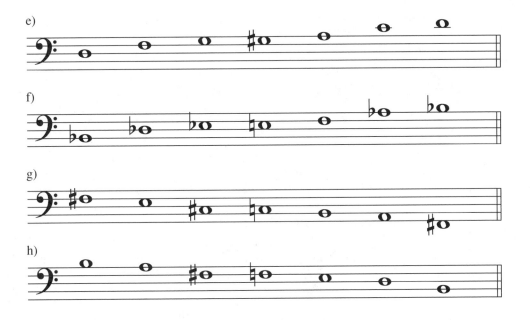

f)

g)

h)

2. Write the following blues scales in the treble clef, ascending only.

a) on G

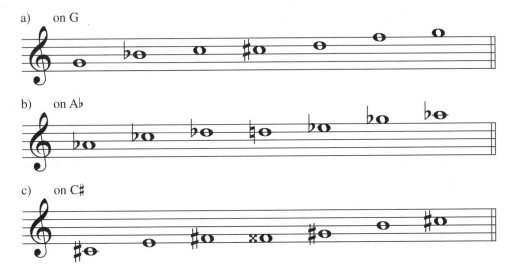

b) on A♭

c) on C♯

3.   Write the following blues scales in the bass clef, descending only.

a)   on E

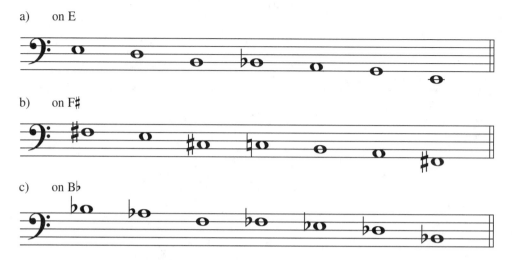

b)   on F♯

c)   on B♭

2   MORE EXERCISES (p. 74)

1.   Write the following blues scales in the given clefs, ascending only.

a)   on D♭

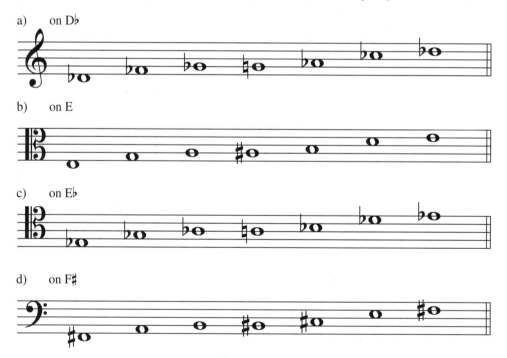

b)   on E

c)   on E♭

d)   on F♯

2. Write the following blues scales in the given clefs, descending only.

a) on A♭

b) on B♭

c) on C♯

d) on B

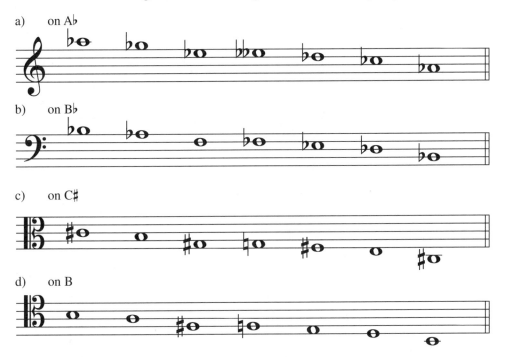

1 2 EXERCISES (p. 76)

1. Add accidentals to each of the following to create octatonic scales. Do not alter the first *two* notes of each scale.

a)

b)

c)

d)

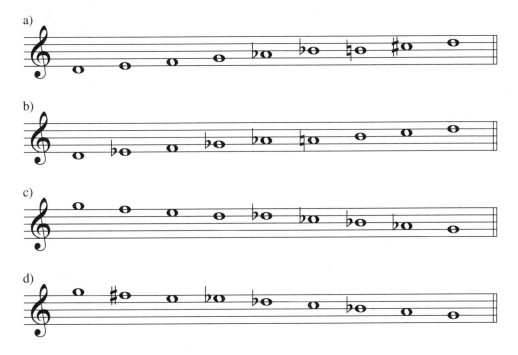

e)

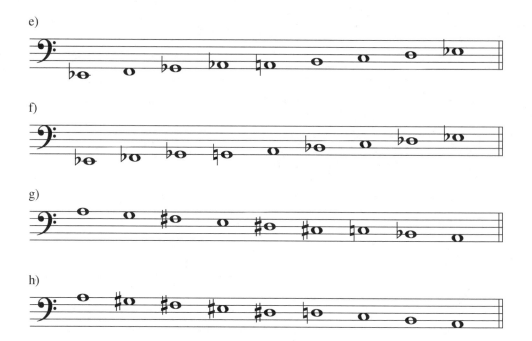

f)

g)

h)

2.   Write each of the following octatonic scales in the bass clef, ascending and descending. (Sample answers. Other spellings are possible.)

a)   on E, starting with a semitone

b)   on F, starting with a whole tone

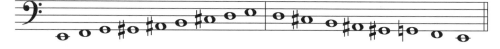

c)   on A♭, starting with a whole tone

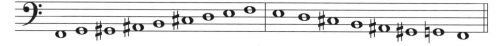

d)   on C♯, starting with a semitone

3. Write each of the following octatonic scales in the treble clef, ascending and descending. (Sample answers. Other spellings are possible.)

a) on B, starting with a whole tone

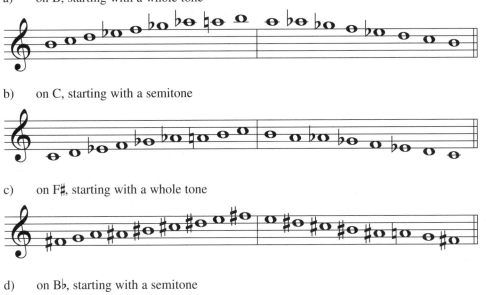

b) on C, starting with a semitone

c) on F♯, starting with a whole tone

d) on B♭, starting with a semitone

2 MORE EXERCISES (p. 78)

1. Complete each of the following octatonic scales. (Sample answers. Other spellings are possible.)

a)

b)

c)

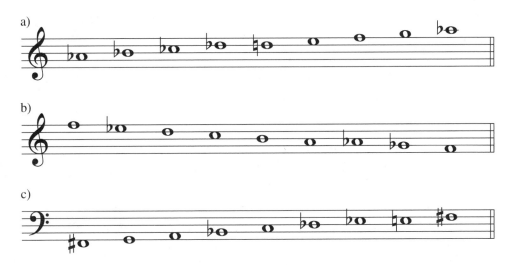

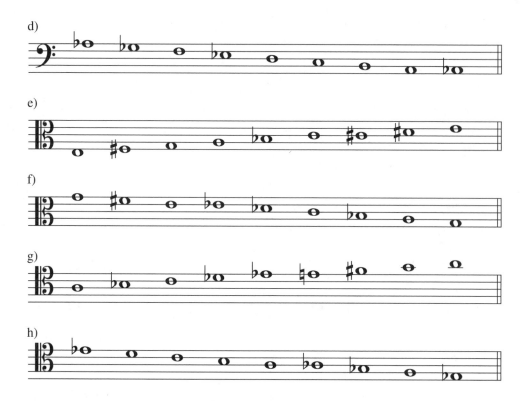

d)

e)

f)

g)

h)

1 2 **EXERCISES** (p. 81)

1. Write the following pentatonic scales in the treble clef, ascending and descending, using accidentals.

a) on G

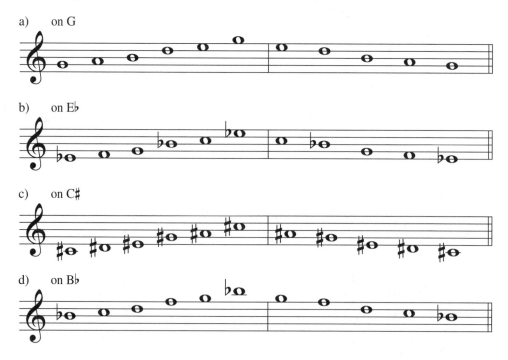

b) on E♭

c) on C♯

d) on B♭

2. Write the following pentatonic scales in the bass clef, ascending and descending, using accidentals.

a) on F

b) on A♭

c) on G♭

d) on E

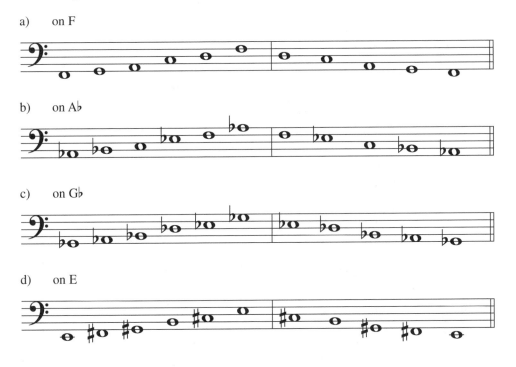

3. Write the following major scales in the treble clef, ascending only, using the correct key signature for each. Then write pentatonic scales starting on the same notes and using the same key signatures.

Example: G major   G pentatonic

a) A major   A pentatonic

b) D♭ major   D♭ pentatonic

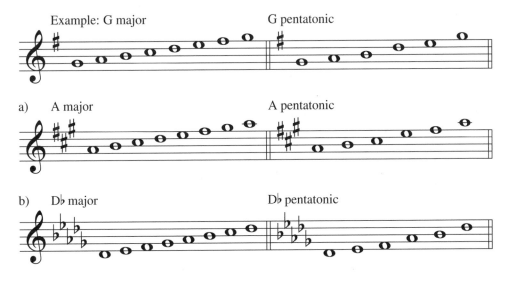

c) F♯ major   F♯ pentatonic

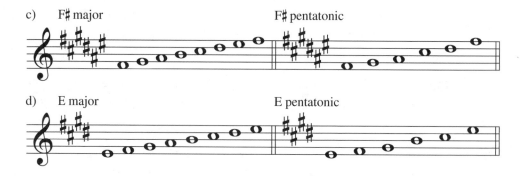

d) E major   E pentatonic

4. Write the following major scales in the bass clef, descending only, using the correct key signature for each. Then write pentatonic scales starting on the same notes and using the same key signatures.

a) D major   D pentatonic

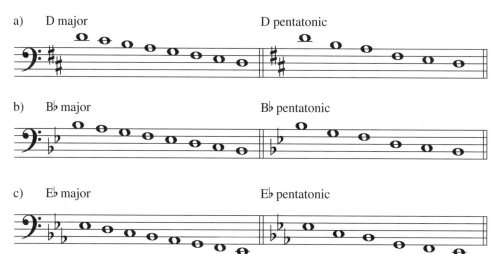

b) B♭ major   B♭ pentatonic

c) E♭ major   E♭ pentatonic

2 MORE EXERCISES (p. 83)

1. Write the following pentatonic scales in the given clefs, ascending and descending, using accidentals.

a) on B

b) on A♭

59

c) on E

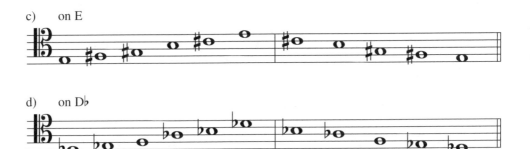

d) on Db

2. Write the following pentatonic scales in the given clefs, ascending and descending, using the key signature of the tonic major scale for each.

a) on Gb

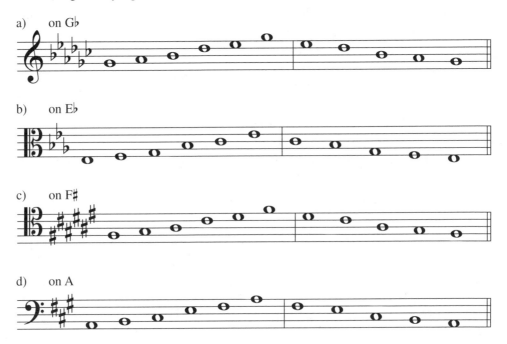

b) on Eb

c) on F#

d) on A

2 EXERCISES (p. 90)

1. Write the following major scales in the given clefs, ascending and descending. Use the correct key signature and start on the specified degree for each scale. Identify the equivalent mode in each case.

Example: A major on $\hat{4}$ or __Lydian mode on D__

a) G major on $\hat{5}$ or __Mixoydian mode on D__

b) B major on $\hat{2}$ or __Dorian mode on C♯__

c) A♭ major on $\hat{3}$ or __Phrygian mode on C__

d) B♭ major on $\hat{2}$ or __Dorian mode on C__

e) D major on $\hat{4}$ or __Lydian mode on G__

f) E♭ major on $\hat{2}$ or __Dorian mode on F__

g) F major on $\hat{4}$ or __Lydian mode on B♭__

h) E major on $\hat{3}$ or __Phrygian mode on G♯__

2. Write the following modes in the given clefs, ascending and descending. Use accidentals instead of key signatures. Identify the equivalent major scale and its starting degree in each case.

Example: Mixolydian mode on B♭ or ___E♭ major on $\hat5$___

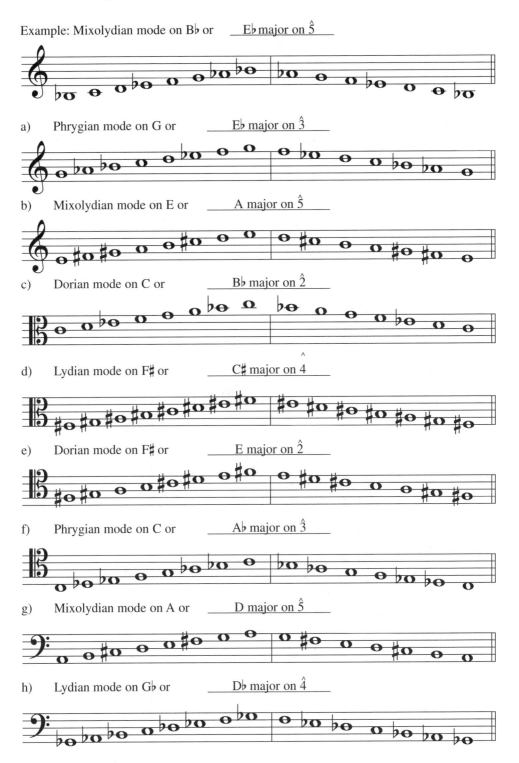

a) Phrygian mode on G or ___E♭ major on $\hat3$___

b) Mixolydian mode on E or ___A major on $\hat5$___

c) Dorian mode on C or ___B♭ major on $\hat2$___

d) Lydian mode on F♯ or ___C♯ major on $\hat4$___

e) Dorian mode on F♯ or ___E major on $\hat2$___

f) Phrygian mode on C or ___A♭ major on $\hat3$___

g) Mixolydian mode on A or ___D major on $\hat5$___

h) Lydian mode on G♭ or ___D♭ major on $\hat4$___

3. Write the following modes in the given clefs, ascending and descending.
    Use key signatures and add any necessary accidentals.

a) Lydian mode on B♭

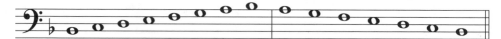

b) Dorian mode on C

c) Mixolydian mode on A♭

d) Phrygian mode on F♯

e) Lydian mode on E

f) Phrygian mode on B♭

g) Dorian mode on E

h) Mixolydian mode on A

1 2   REVIEW: IDENTIFYING SCALE TYPES

EXERCISES (p. 93)

1.   Name each of the following scales as major, natural minor, harmonic minor, melodic minor, whole tone, chromatic, blues, octatonic, or pentatonic.

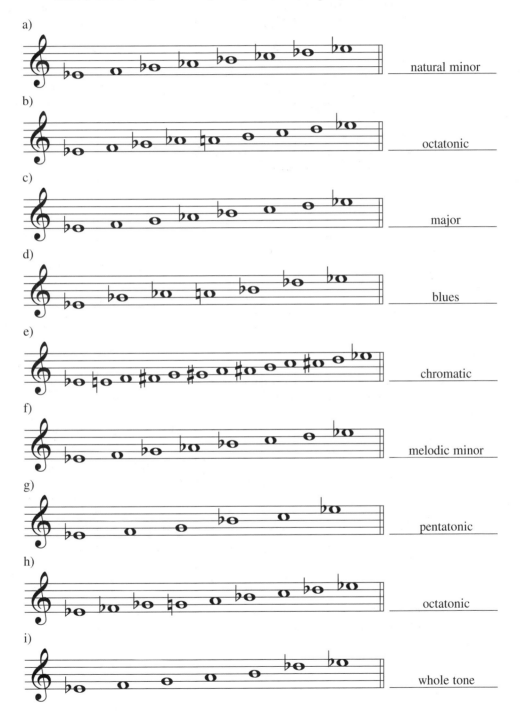

a) natural minor

b) octatonic

c) major

d) blues

e) chromatic

f) melodic minor

g) pentatonic

h) octatonic

i) whole tone

64

2. Name each of the following scales as major, natural minor, harmonic minor, melodic minor, whole tone, chromatic, blues, octatonic, or pentatonic.

a)

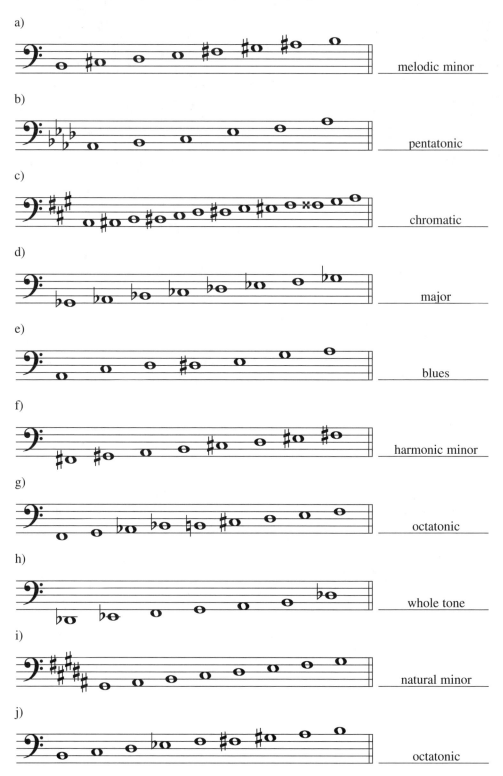

melodic minor

b)

pentatonic

c)

chromatic

d)

major

e)

blues

f)

harmonic minor

g)

octatonic

h)

whole tone

i)

natural minor

j)

octatonic

3. Name each of the following scales as major, natural minor, harmonic minor, melodic minor, whole tone, chromatic, blues, octatonic, or pentatonic.

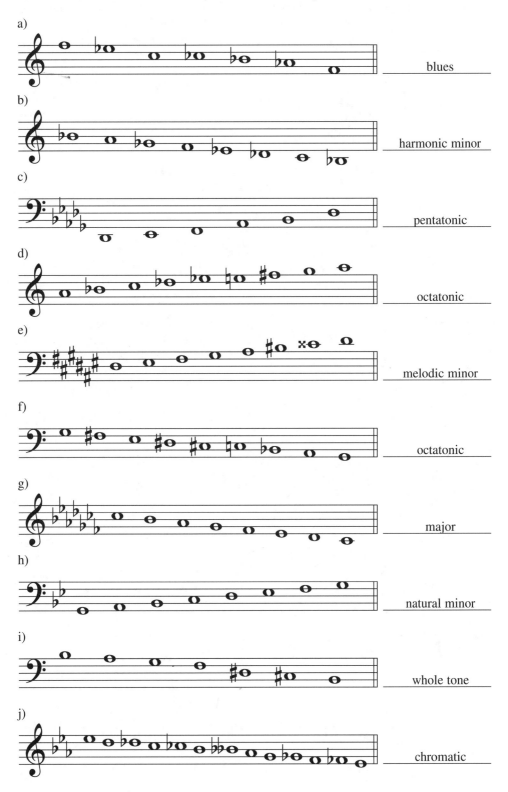

a) _____ blues

b) _____ harmonic minor

c) _____ pentatonic

d) _____ octatonic

e) _____ melodic minor

f) _____ octatonic

g) _____ major

h) _____ natural minor

i) _____ whole tone

j) _____ chromatic

2 MORE EXERCISES (p. 96)

1. Identify each of the following as major, minor (specify natural, harmonic, or melodic), whole tone, chromatic, blues, octatonic, or pentatonic scales, or as Dorian, Phrygian, Lydian, or Mixolydian modes. Assume that each example starts on its tonic.

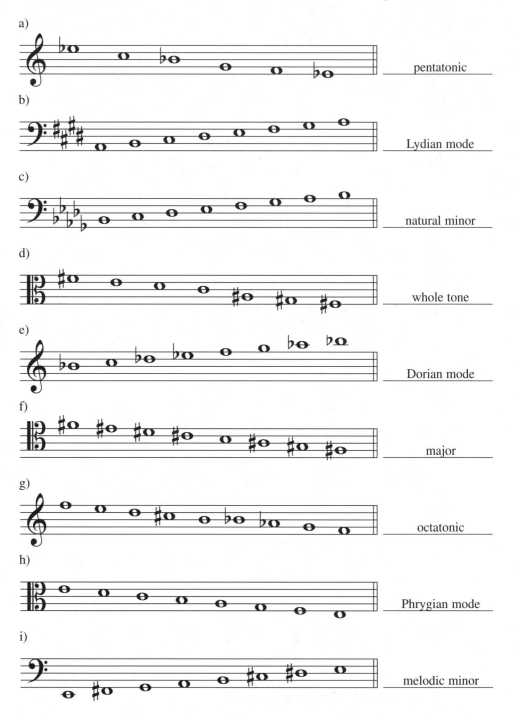

a) pentatonic

b) Lydian mode

c) natural minor

d) whole tone

e) Dorian mode

f) major

g) octatonic

h) Phrygian mode

i) melodic minor

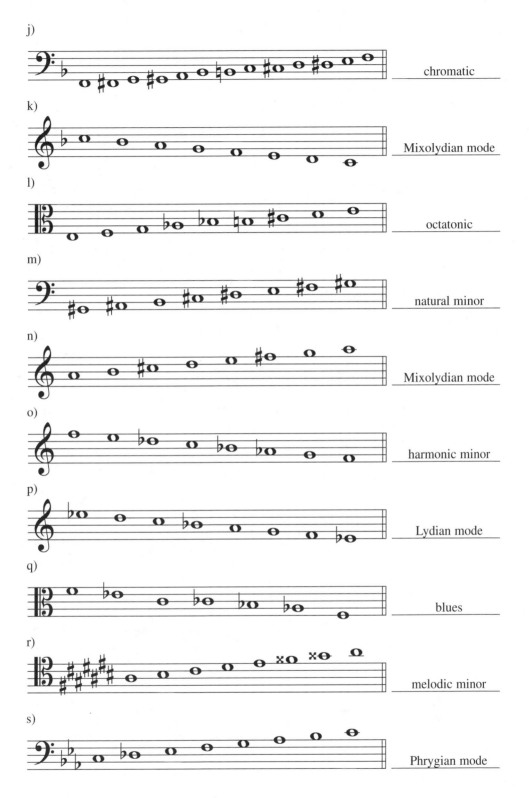

67

68

CHAPTER 4

INTERVALS

P 1   EXERCISES (p. 101)

1.   Name the following intervals. Use abbreviations: maj for major, min for minor, and per for perfect.

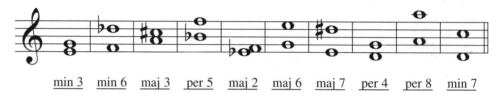

min 3   min 6   maj 3   per 5   maj 2   maj 6   maj 7   per 4   per 8   min 7

2.   Write the following intervals above the given notes.

3.   Name the following intervals.

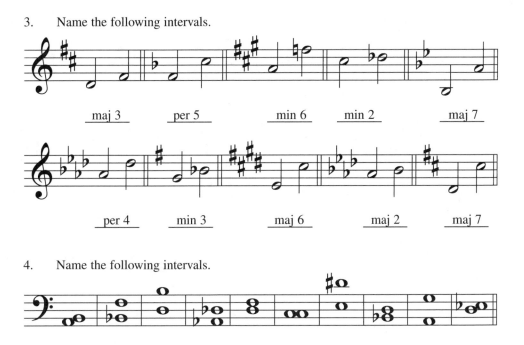

maj 3   per 5   min 6   min 2   maj 7

per 4   min 3   maj 6   maj 2   maj 7

4.   Name the following intervals.

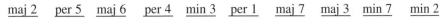

maj 2   per 5   maj 6   per 4   min 3   per 1   maj 7   maj 3   min 7   min 2

5.   Write the following intervals above the given notes.

a)   maj 3   per 5   min 3   maj 6   min 2   per 4   min 6   per 1

b)   maj 3   per 5   min 3   maj 6   min 2   per 4   min 6   per 1

c)   maj 3   per 5   min 3   maj 6   min 2   per 4   min 6   per 1

d)   maj 3   per 5   min 3   maj 6   min 2   per 4   min 6   per 1

e) maj 3 | per 5 | min 3 | maj 6 | min 2 | per 4 | min 6 | per 1

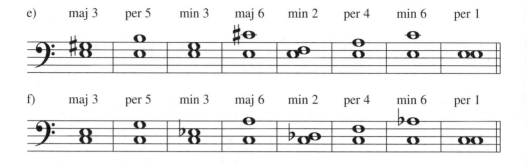

f) maj 3 | per 5 | min 3 | maj 6 | min 2 | per 4 | min 6 | per 1

6. Name the following intervals.

per 4   min 3   maj 7   min 6   per 5

min 7   maj 2   min 7   per 1   maj 6

1 2 EXERCISES (p. 107)

1. Write the following intervals above the given notes.

a) maj 2 | aug 6 | dim 5 | aug 1 | per 5 | min 3 | dim 4 | aug 7

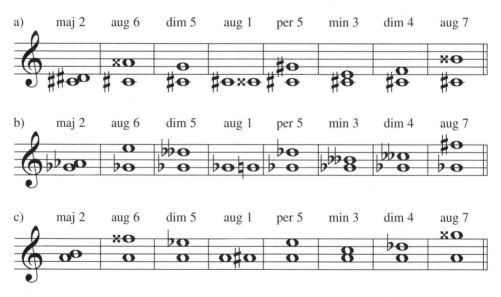

b) maj 2 | aug 6 | dim 5 | aug 1 | per 5 | min 3 | dim 4 | aug 7

c) maj 2 | aug 6 | dim 5 | aug 1 | per 5 | min 3 | dim 4 | aug 7

2. Write the following intervals above the given notes.

72

3.   Name the following intervals. Invert them on the staff directly underneath and name the inversions.

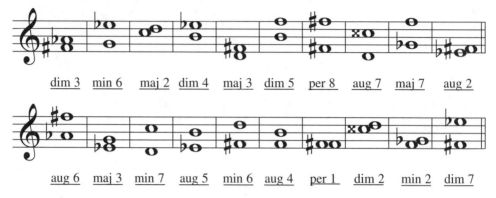

dim 3   min 6   maj 2   dim 4   maj 3   dim 5   per 8   aug 7   maj 7   aug 2

aug 6   maj 3   min 7   aug 5   min 6   aug 4   per 1   dim 2   min 2   dim 7

4.   Name the following intervals. Invert them and name the inversions.

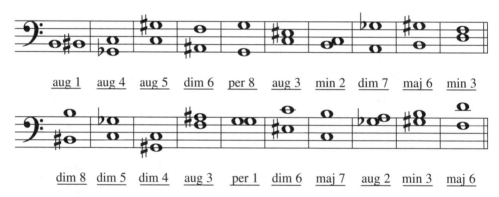

aug 1   aug 4   aug 5   dim 6   per 8   aug 3   min 2   dim 7   maj 6   min 3

dim 8   dim 5   dim 4   aug 3   per 1   dim 6   maj 7   aug 2   min 3   maj 6

5.   Write the following intervals above the given notes. Invert them and name the inversions.

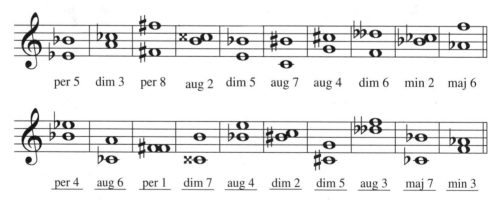

per 5   dim 3   per 8   aug 2   dim 5   aug 7   aug 4   dim 6   min 2   maj 6

per 4   aug 6   per 1   dim 7   aug 4   dim 2   dim 5   aug 3   maj 7   min 3

6. Write the following intervals above the given notes. Invert them and name the inversions.

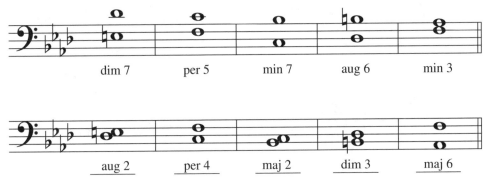

dim 7   per 5   min 7   aug 6   min 3

aug 2   per 4   maj 2   dim 3   maj 6

7. Name the following intervals. Invert them in the bass clef and name the inversions.

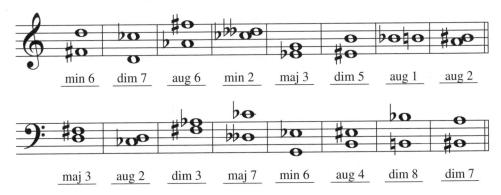

min 6   dim 7   aug 6   min 2   maj 3   dim 5   aug 1   aug 2

maj 3   aug 2   dim 3   maj 7   min 6   aug 4   dim 8   dim 7

2   EXERCISES (p. 113)

1. Name the following intervals.

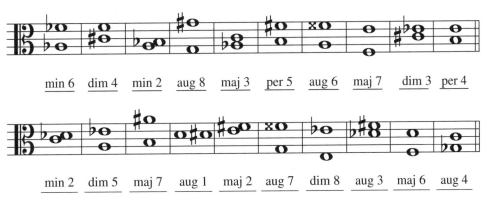

min 6   dim 4   min 2   aug 8   maj 3   per 5   aug 6   maj 7   dim 3   per 4

min 2   dim 5   maj 7   aug 1   maj 2   aug 7   dim 8   aug 3   maj 6   aug 4

2.   Name the following intervals.

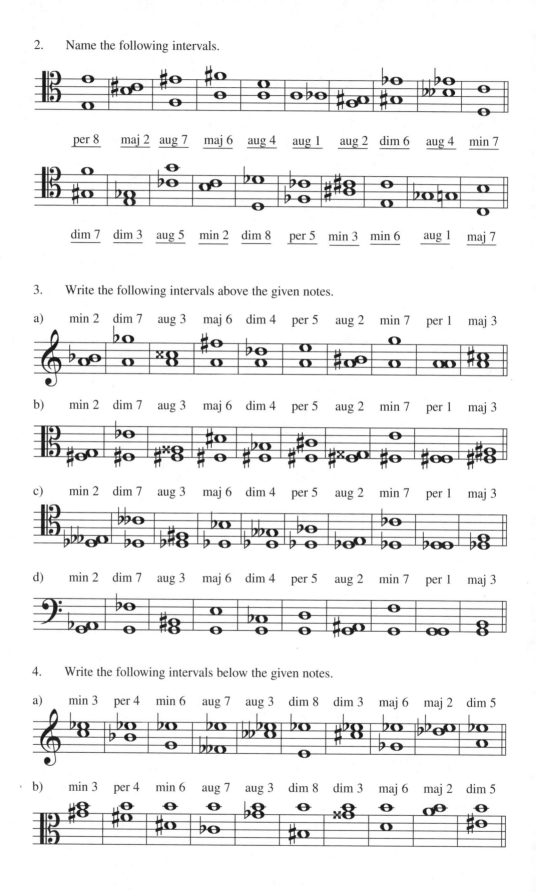

per 8   maj 2   aug 7   maj 6   aug 4   aug 1   aug 2   dim 6   aug 4   min 7

dim 7   dim 3   aug 5   min 2   dim 8   per 5   min 3   min 6   aug 1   maj 7

3.   Write the following intervals above the given notes.

a)   min 2   dim 7   aug 3   maj 6   dim 4   per 5   aug 2   min 7   per 1   maj 3

b)   min 2   dim 7   aug 3   maj 6   dim 4   per 5   aug 2   min 7   per 1   maj 3

c)   min 2   dim 7   aug 3   maj 6   dim 4   per 5   aug 2   min 7   per 1   maj 3

d)   min 2   dim 7   aug 3   maj 6   dim 4   per 5   aug 2   min 7   per 1   maj 3

4.   Write the following intervals below the given notes.

a)   min 3   per 4   min 6   aug 7   aug 3   dim 8   dim 3   maj 6   maj 2   dim 5

b)   min 3   per 4   min 6   aug 7   aug 3   dim 8   dim 3   maj 6   maj 2   dim 5

c) min 3   per 4   min 6   aug 7   aug 3   dim 8   dim 3   maj 6   maj 2   dim 5

d) min 3   per 4   min 6   aug 7   aug 3   dim 8   dim 3   maj 6   maj 2   dim 5

5.   Name the following intervals. Invert them in the alto clef and name the inversions.

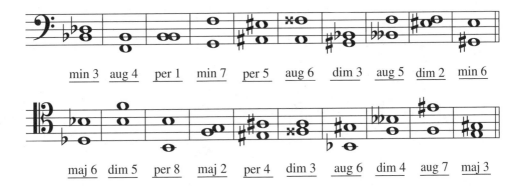

aug 3   dim 5   maj 6   dim 3   dim 8   maj 2   dim 7   per 4   aug 2   dim 6

dim 6   aug 4   min 3   aug 6   aug 1   min 7   aug 2   per 5   dim 7   aug 3

6.   Name the following intervals. Invert them in the tenor clef and name the inversions.

min 3   aug 4   per 1   min 7   per 5   aug 6   dim 3   aug 5   dim 2   min 6

maj 6   dim 5   per 8   maj 2   per 4   dim 3   aug 6   dim 4   aug 7   maj 3

7. Name the following intervals. Change the upper note of each enharmonically and rename the intervals.

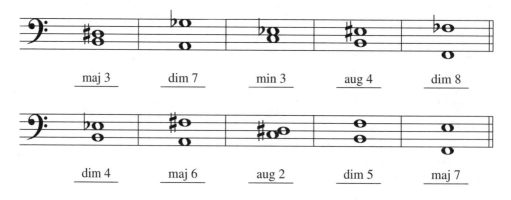

maj 3 dim 7 min 3 aug 4 dim 8

dim 4 maj 6 aug 2 dim 5 maj 7

8. Name the following intervals. Change the lower note of each enharmonically and rename the intervals.

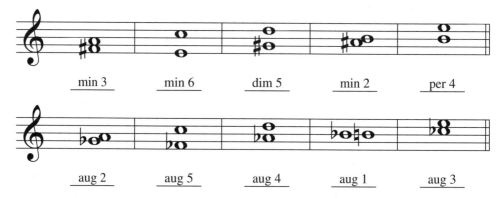

min 3 min 6 dim 5 min 2 per 4

aug 2 aug 5 aug 4 aug 1 aug 3

9. Name the following compound intervals. Invert them and name the inversions.

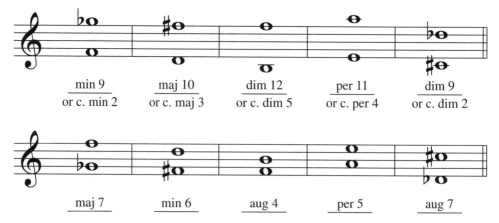

min 9   maj 10   dim 12   per 11   dim 9
or c. min 2   or c. maj 3   or c. dim 5   or c. per 4   or c. dim 2

maj 7   min 6   aug 4   per 5   aug 7

10. Name the following compound intervals. Invert them and name the inversions.

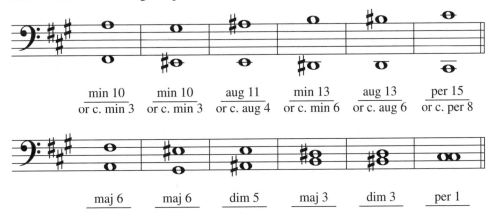

min 10	min 10	aug 11	min 13	aug 13	per 15
or c. min 3	or c. min 3	or c. aug 4	or c. min 6	or c. aug 6	or c. per 8

maj 6	maj 6	dim 5	maj 3	dim 3	per 1

11. Name the following compound intervals. Invert them in the treble clef and name the inversions.

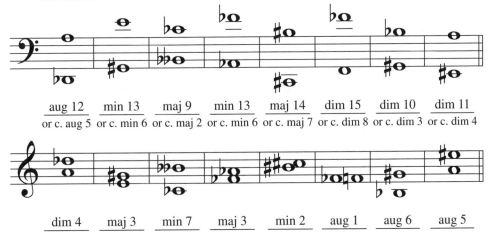

aug 12	min 13	maj 9	min 13	maj 14	dim 15	dim 10	dim 11
or c. aug 5	or c. min 6	or c. maj 2	or c. min 6	or c. maj 7	or c. dim 8	or c. dim 3	or c. dim 4

dim 4	maj 3	min 7	maj 3	min 2	aug 1	aug 6	aug 5

12. Name the following intervals.

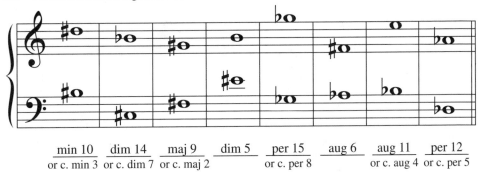

min 10	dim 14	maj 9	dim 5	per 15	aug 6	aug 11	per 12
or c. min 3	or c. dim 7	or c. maj 2		or c. per 8		or c. aug 4	or c. per 5

78

13. Name the intervals between successive notes of the following.

per 4   dim 5   maj 3   min 6   maj 2   min 7   aug 4   maj 2   dim 7   dim 8

14. Write three different major 3rds that are found in the scale of E♭ major.

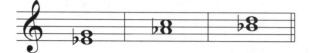

15. Write three different major 6ths that are found in the scale of F minor, natural form.

16. Name all the scales (major, natural minor, and harmonic minor) in which each of these intervals may be found.

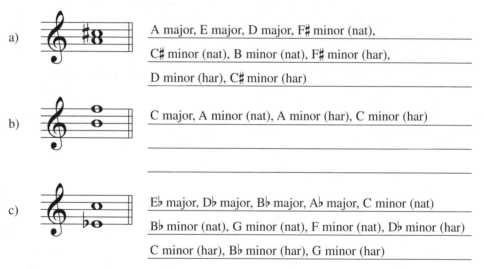

a) A major, E major, D major, F♯ minor (nat), C♯ minor (nat), B minor (nat), F♯ minor (har), D minor (har), C♯ minor (har)

b) C major, A minor (nat), A minor (har), C minor (har)

c) E♭ major, D♭ major, B♭ major, A♭ major, C minor (nat) B♭ minor (nat), G minor (nat), F minor (nat), D♭ minor (har) C minor (har), B♭ minor (har), G minor (har)

17. Write a diminished 7th that is found in the scale of G harmonic minor.

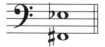

18.   Write three different perfect 4ths that are found in the scale of B major.

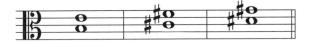

19.   Write three different minor 2nds that are found in the scale of C♯ harmonic minor.

20.   Write four different major 2nds that are found in the scale of A major.

or

21.   Write the augmented 2nd that is found in the scale of G♯ harmonic minor.

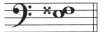

22.   Write the augmented 5th that is found in the scale of B harmonic minor.

23.   Write four different minor 3rds that are found in the scale of E minor, natural form.

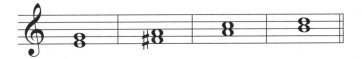

24.   Mark three major 3rds that occur between the different notes of this scale.

25. Name all the scales (major, natural minor, and harmonic minor) in which each of the following intervals is found.

a)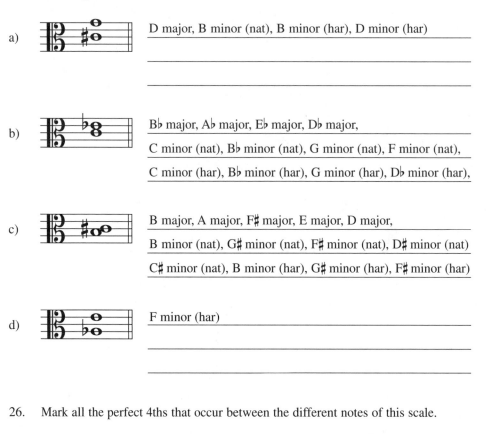

D major, B minor (nat), B minor (har), D minor (har)

b)

B♭ major, A♭ major, E♭ major, D♭ major,

C minor (nat), B♭ minor (nat), G minor (nat), F minor (nat),

C minor (har), B♭ minor (har), G minor (har), D♭ minor (har),

c)

B major, A major, F♯ major, E major, D major,

B minor (nat), G♯ minor (nat), F♯ minor (nat), D♯ minor (nat)

C♯ minor (nat), B minor (har), G♯ minor (har), F♯ minor (har)

d)

F minor (har)

26. Mark all the perfect 4ths that occur between the different notes of this scale.

27. Name the following intervals. Name the one scale that contains them all.

Scale:

F♯ minor (harmonic)

per 4   aug 5   min 2   maj 6   maj 7

28. Name the following intervals. Name *two* scales that contain them all.

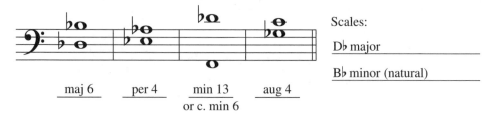

Scales:

D♭ major

B♭ minor (natural)

maj 6   per 4   min 13   aug 4
                 or c. min 6

CHAPTER 5

CHORDS

P 1 2   EXERCISES (p. 122)

1.   Write the following triads in the treble clef, using the correct key signature for each.

    a) the dominant triad of A major

    b) the tonic triad of F major

    c) the subdominant triad of E♭ major

    d) the tonic triad of G major

    e) the dominant triad of E major

    f) the subdominant triad of D major

2.   Write the following triads in the bass clef, using the correct key signature for each.

    a) the dominant triad of C minor

    b) the tonic triad of D minor

    c) the dominant triad of F♯ minor

    d) the subdominant triad of E minor

    e) the dominant triad of F minor

    f) the subdominant triad of C♯ minor

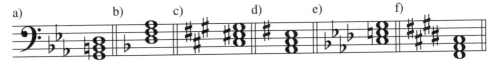

3.   Write the following triads in the treble clef, using accidentals instead of a key signature.

    a) the tonic triad of B minor

    b) the dominant triad of C♯ minor

    c) the subdominant triad of F♯ minor

    d) the dominant triad of G minor

    e) the subdominant triad of A minor

    f) the dominant triad of D minor

    g) the tonic triad of C minor

    h) the dominant triad of E minor

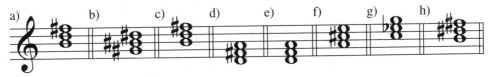

4. Write the following triads in the bass clef, using accidentals instead of a key signature.

    a) the tonic triad of A♭ major

    b) the dominant triad of C major

    c) the subdominant triad of B♭ major

    d) the dominant triad of D major

    e) the tonic triad of E♭ major

    f) the subdominant triad of A major

    g) the dominant triad of G major

    h) the subdominant triad of E major

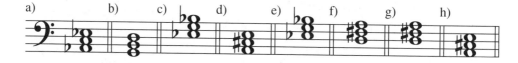

5. For each of the following, name the *major* key and identify the triad as tonic, subdominant, or dominant.

major key: E♭ major   G major   E major   B♭ major   C major   A major

triad: dominant subdominant   tonic   subdominant dominant   tonic

6. For each of the following, name the *minor* key and identify the triad as tonic, subdominant, or dominant.

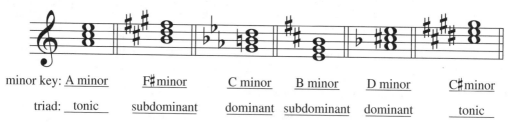

minor key: A minor   F♯ minor   C minor   B minor   D minor   C♯ minor

triad: tonic   subdominant   dominant subdominant   dominant   tonic

7. Fill in the blanks.

a) is the tonic triad of the key of __C minor__ .

b) is the dominant triad of the keys of _D major_ and _D minor_ .

c) is the subdominant triad of the key of __B minor__.

d) is the tonic triad of the key of __G minor__.

e) is the dominant triad of the keys of __G major__ and __G minor__.

8. Fill in the blanks.

a) is the ___dominant___ triad in the key of ___G minor___.

b) is the ___subdominant___ triad in the key of ___E major___.

c) is the ___tonic___ triad in the key of ___E♭ major___.

d) is the ___dominant___ triad in the key of ___E minor___.

e) is the ___subdominant___ triad in the key of ___F minor___.

1 2 EXERCISES (p. 126)

1. Write a major triad and its inversions, using each of the following notes as the root.

2.   Write a minor triad and its inversions, using each of the following notes as the root.

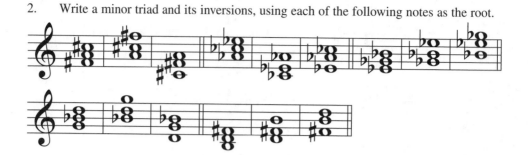

3.   Solve the following triads.

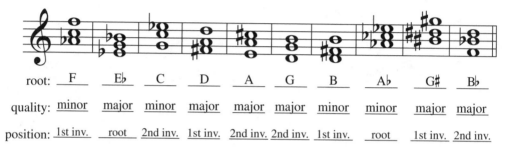

root:	F	E♭	C	D	A	G	B	A♭	G♯	B♭
quality:	minor	major	minor	major	major	major	minor	minor	major	major
position:	1st inv.	root	2nd inv.	1st inv.	2nd inv.	2nd inv.	1st inv.	root	1st inv.	2nd inv.

4.   Write the following triads in the treble clef.

   a) the root position of the F major triad

   b) the root position of the D minor triad

   c) the first inversion of the G major triad

   d) the second inversion of the E minor triad

   e) the root position of the B♭ minor triad

   f) the second inversion of the C major triad

   g) the first inversion of the A♭ major triad

   h) the second inversion of the G♯ minor triad

   i) the root position of the B major triad

   j) the first inversion of the D major triad

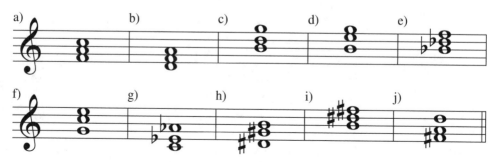

5. Write the following triads in root position in the bass clef.

    a) a major triad with F as the root
    b) a minor triad with D as the fifth
    c) a minor triad with C as the third
    d) a major triad with G as the third
    e) a major triad with A♭ as the root
    f) a minor triad with A as the fifth
    g) a major triad with B as the fifth
    h) a minor triad with E♭ as the third
    i) a minor triad with B as the root
    j) a major triad with C♯ as the third

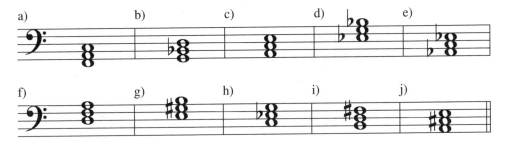

6. Add accidentals where necessary to make each of these a major triad.*

7. Add accidentals where necessary to make each of these a minor triad.*

* Different accidentals from those used are also acceptable.

8. Write the following triads in the treble clef, using the correct key signature for each.

    a) the mediant triad of E♭ major, in root position
    b) the dominant triad of B♭ minor, in second inversion
    c) the tonic triad of E major, in first inversion
    d) the subdominant triad of F minor, in second inversion
    e) the supertonic triad of B major, in root position

9. Write the following triads in the bass clef, using the accidentals instead of key signatures.

   a) the tonic triad of A major, in first inversion

   b) the submediant triad of G♭ major, in root position

   c) the subdominant triad of C minor, in second inversion

   d) the dominant triad of F♯ minor, in first inversion

   e) the supertonic triad of B♭ major, in root position

10. Identify the root, quality, and position of each of the following triads. Then name the major key of each and the technical degree of the root.

    Example:

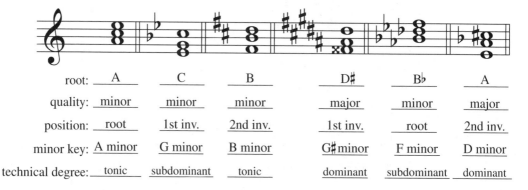

root:	A♭	A	A♭	G♯	B♭	G
quality:	major	minor	major	minor	major	major
position:	2nd inv.	root	1st inv.	root	1st inv.	2nd inv.
major key:	D♭ major	G major	A♭ major	B major	F major	D major
technical degree:	dominant	supertonic	tonic	submediant	subdominant	subdominant

11. Identify the root, quality, and position of each of the following triads. Then name the minor key of each and the technical degree of the root.

root:	A	C	B	D♯	B♭	A
quality:	minor	minor	minor	major	minor	major
position:	root	1st inv.	2nd inv.	1st inv.	root	2nd inv.
minor key:	A minor	G minor	B minor	G♯ minor	F minor	D minor
technical degree:	tonic	subdominant	tonic	dominant	subdominant	dominant

2 EXERCISES (p. 130)

1. Solve the following triads.

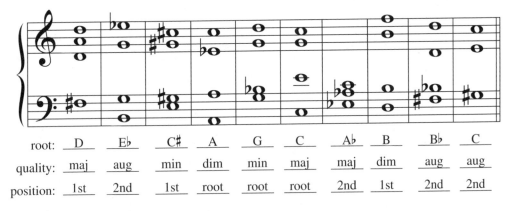

root:	D	E♭	C♯	A	G	C	A♭	B	B♭	C
quality:	maj	aug	min	dim	min	maj	maj	dim	aug	aug
position:	1st	2nd	1st	root	root	root	2nd	1st	2nd	2nd

2. Write the following triads in root position in the treble clef. Use close position.

    a) an augmented triad with D as the third

    b) a diminished triad with C♭ as the fifth

    c) a diminished triad with C♯ as the root

    d) an augmented triad with E♭ as the root

    e) an augmented triad with D as the fifth

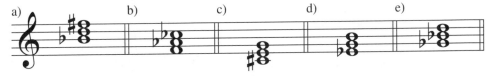

3. Write three different arrangements of each of the following triads in open position. (Sample answers. Other arrangements are possible.)

    a) the root position of the major triad of A♭

    b) the second inversion of the minor triad of F

    c) the first inversion of the minor triad of C

    d) the root position of the augmented triad of B

    e) the first inversion of the minor triad of F♯

    f) the second inversion of the diminished triad of E

    g) the first inversion of the augmented triad of A

    h) the root position of the diminished triad of C♯

    i) the second inversion of the major triad of D♭

    j) the first inversion of the minor triad of G

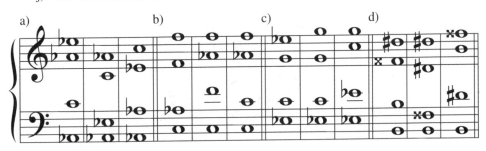

88

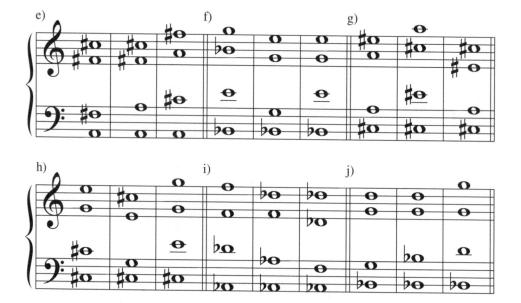

4. Write the four different kinds of triads in root position *below* each of the following notes.

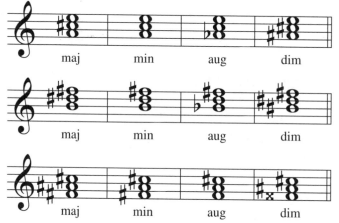

5. Write the four different kinds of triads in root position *above* each of the following notes.

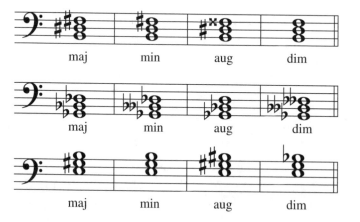

2   EXERCISES (p. 135)

1.   Write and name all the triads found in the A major scale.

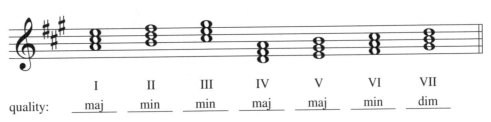

	I	II	III	IV	V	VI	VII
quality:	maj	min	min	maj	maj	min	dim

2.   Write and name all the triads found in the E♭ major scale.

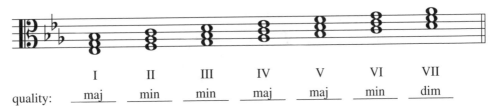

	I	II	III	IV	V	VI	VII
quality:	maj	min	min	maj	maj	min	dim

3.   (a) Write and name all the triads found in the F minor scale, harmonic form.

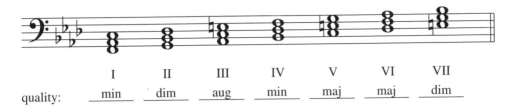

	I	II	III	IV	V	VI	VII
quality:	min	dim	aug	min	maj	maj	dim

(b) Write and name all the triads found in the F minor scale, natural form.

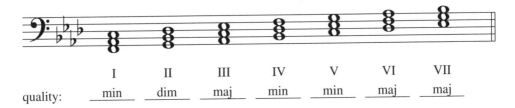

	I	II	III	IV	V	VI	VII
quality:	min	dim	maj	min	min	maj	maj

4.   (a) Write and name all the triads found in the G minor scale, harmonic form.

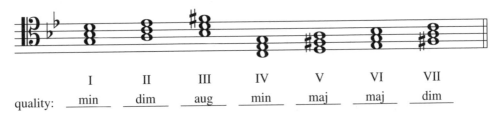

	I	II	III	IV	V	VI	VII
quality:	min	dim	aug	min	maj	maj	dim

(b) Write and name all the triads found in the G minor scale, natural form.

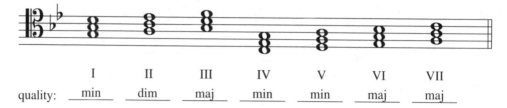

	I	II	III	IV	V	VI	VII
quality:	min	dim	maj	min	min	maj	maj

5. Name all the scales (major, harmonic minor, and natural minor) in which each of the following triads is found.

(a) 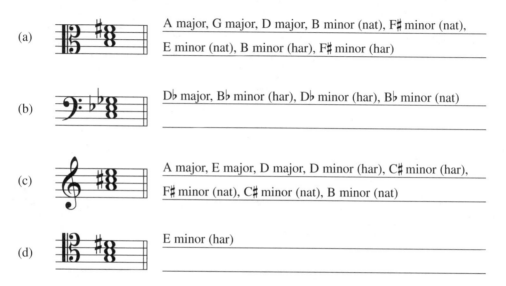 A major, G major, D major, B minor (nat), F♯ minor (nat), E minor (nat), B minor (har), F♯ minor (har)

(b) D♭ major, B♭ minor (har), D♭ minor (har), B♭ minor (nat)

(c) A major, E major, D major, D minor (har), C♯ minor (har), F♯ minor (nat), C♯ minor (nat), B minor (nat)

(d) E minor (har)

6. Write the triad that is found only in the G minor harmonic scale.

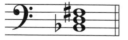

7. Write the triad that is common only to these scales: B♭ major, G minor (harmonic and natural forms), and B♭ minor (harmonic form only).

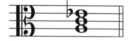

8. Name all the scales (major, harmonic minor, and natural minor) in which each of the following triads is found.

(a) 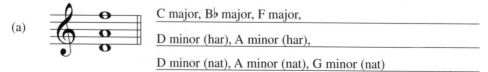 C major, B♭ major, F major,

D minor (har), A minor (har),

D minor (nat), A minor (nat), G minor (nat)

(b)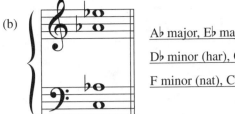

Ab major, Eb major, Db major,

Db minor (har), C minor (har),

F minor (nat), C minor (nat), Bb minor (nat)

9.   Write the triad that is common only to these scales: Db major, Bb minor (harmonic and natural forms), Gb major, F minor (harmonic and natural forms), Ab major, and Eb minor (natural form only).

10.   In the treble clef, write the diminished triads that are found in the following scales:
a) D major b) Ab major c) B major d) E major e) Db major

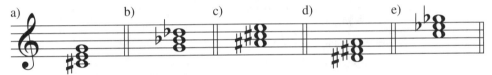

11.   In the bass clef, write the augmented triads that are found in the following harmonic minor scales: a) B minor b) G# minor c) C minor d) F minor e) D minor

12.   Write the following triads in close position in the treble clef, using the proper key signature for each. Name the quality of each triad.

a) the mediant triad of F minor, natural form, in root position
b) the leading-note triad of G# minor, harmonic form, in second inversion
c) the subdominant triad of E minor, in first inversion
d) the dominant triad of Bb minor, natural form, in first inversion
e) the tonic triad of Ab minor, in second inversion
f) the mediant triad of C minor, harmonic form, in first inversion
g) the subtonic triad of C# minor, natural form, in second inversion
h) the dominant triad of D# minor, harmonic form, in root position

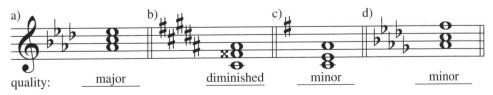

quality: major   diminished   minor   minor

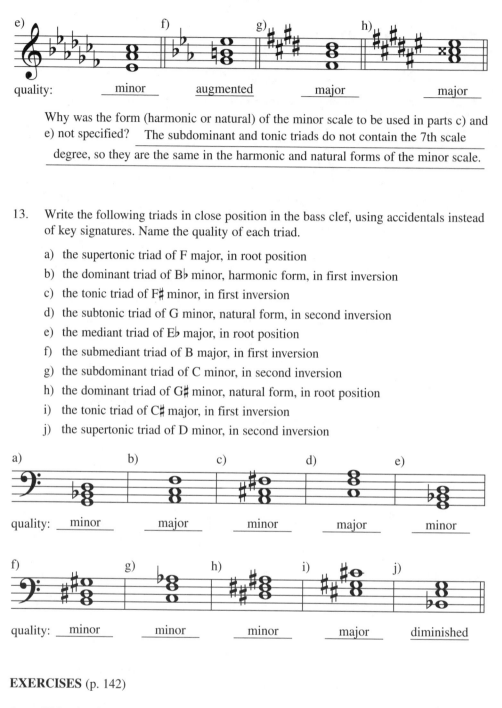

quality: __minor__   __augmented__   __major__   __major__

Why was the form (harmonic or natural) of the minor scale to be used in parts c) and e) not specified?   The subdominant and tonic triads do not contain the 7th scale degree, so they are the same in the harmonic and natural forms of the minor scale.

13. Write the following triads in close position in the bass clef, using accidentals instead of key signatures. Name the quality of each triad.

   a) the supertonic triad of F major, in root position
   b) the dominant triad of B♭ minor, harmonic form, in first inversion
   c) the tonic triad of F♯ minor, in first inversion
   d) the subtonic triad of G minor, natural form, in second inversion
   e) the mediant triad of E♭ major, in root position
   f) the submediant triad of B major, in first inversion
   g) the subdominant triad of C minor, in second inversion
   h) the dominant triad of G♯ minor, natural form, in root position
   i) the tonic triad of C♯ major, in first inversion
   j) the supertonic triad of D minor, in second inversion

quality: __minor__   __major__   __minor__   __major__   __minor__

quality: __minor__   __minor__   __minor__   __major__   __diminished__

2 EXERCISES (p. 142)

1. Write the dominant 7th chord and its inversions in each of the following keys, using the correct key signature for each.

a)   A major

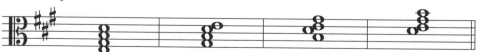

93

2. Solve the following dominant 7th chords.

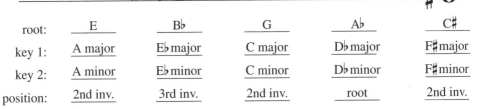

	a)	b)	c)	d)	e)
root:	E	B♭	G	A♭	C♯
key 1:	A major	E♭ major	C major	D♭ major	F♯ major
key 2:	A minor	E♭ minor	C minor	D♭ minor	F♯ minor
position:	2nd inv.	3rd inv.	2nd inv.	root	2nd inv.

94

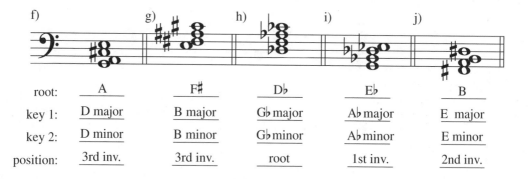

root:	A	F♯	D♭	E♭	B
key 1:	D major	B major	G♭ major	A♭ major	E major
key 2:	D minor	B minor	G♭ minor	A♭ minor	E minor
position:	3rd inv.	3rd inv.	root	1st inv.	2nd inv.

3. Write the following dominant 7ths in the treble clef, using the correct key signature for each.

   a) the first inversion of the dominant 7th of D minor

   b) the second inversion of the dominant 7th of F♯ minor

   c) the root position of the dominant 7th of B major

   d) the third inversion of the dominant 7th of G minor

   e) the root position of the dominant 7th of E♭ major

   f) the first inversion of the dominant 7th of C♯ minor

   g) the second inversion of the dominant 7th of A major

   h) the root position of the dominant 7th of G♭ major

   i) the third inversion of the dominant 7th of G♯ minor

   j) the second inversion of the dominant 7th of D♭ major

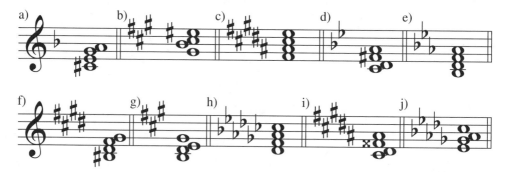

4. Write the dominant 7th and inversions of other dominant 7ths, using F as the lowest note in each case. Name the major key of each.

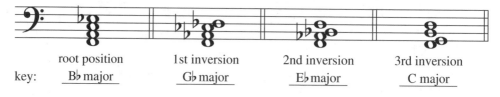

	root position	1st inversion	2nd inversion	3rd inversion
key:	B♭ major	G♭ major	E♭ major	C major

5. Add accidentals to the following to make them into dominant 7th chords. Name the minor key of each. (Alternate accidentals and keys are possible.)

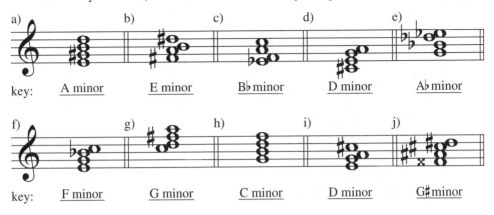

key: A minor   E minor   B♭ minor   D minor   A♭ minor

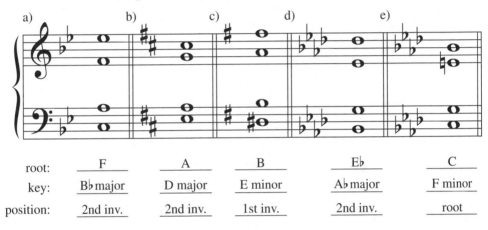

key: F minor   G minor   C minor   D minor   G♯ minor

6. Solve the following dominant 7th chords.

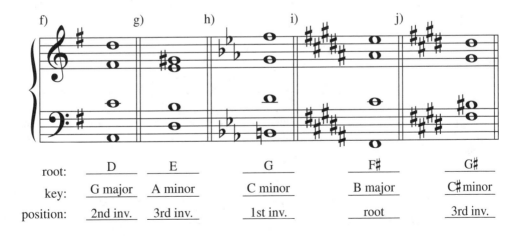

root: F   A   B   E♭   C
key: B♭ major   D major   E minor   A♭ major   F minor
position: 2nd inv.   2nd inv.   1st inv.   2nd inv.   root

root: D   E   G   F♯   G♯
key: G major   A minor   C minor   B major   C♯ minor
position: 2nd inv. 3rd inv.   1st inv.   root   3rd inv.

7.   Write the dominant 7th and inversions of other dominant 7ths, using E as the lowest note for each. Name two keys for each.

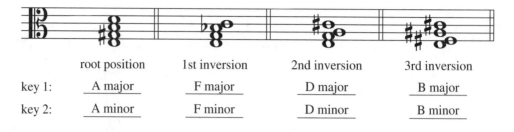

	root position	1st inversion	2nd inversion	3rd inversion
key 1:	A major	F major	D major	B major
key 2:	A minor	F minor	D minor	B minor

8.   Write the dominant 7th and inversions of other dominant 7ths, using G as the lowest note for each. Name the minor key of each.

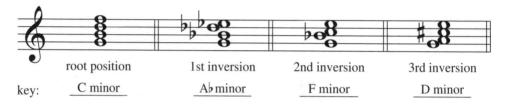

	root position	1st inversion	2nd inversion	3rd inversion
key:	C minor	A♭ minor	F minor	D minor

9.   Write the dominant 7th and inversions of other dominant 7ths, using A as the lowest note of each. Name two keys for each.

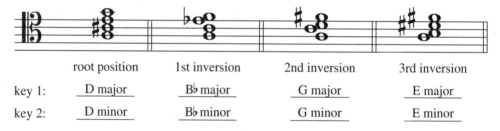

	root position	1st inversion	2nd inversion	3rd inversion
key 1:	D major	B♭ major	G major	E major
key 2:	D minor	B♭ minor	G minor	E minor

2   EXERCISES (p. 148)

1.   Name each of the following chords as: triad, seventh chord, quartal chord, polychord, or cluster. For the triads, also state the quality. Indicate any seventh chords that are dominant 7ths as "V⁷." Triads and seventh chords may appear in root position or in any inversion.

Example:

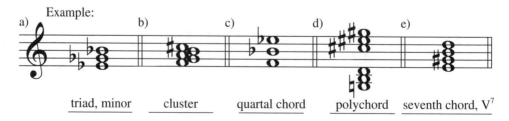

a)	b)	c)	d)	e)
triad, minor	cluster	quartal chord	polychord	seventh chord, V^7

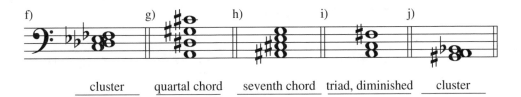

cluster   quartal chord   seventh chord   triad, diminished   cluster

2.   See instructions for Exercise 1.

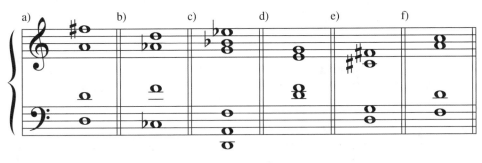

triad, major   seventh chord   polychord   cluster   quartal chord   seventh chord

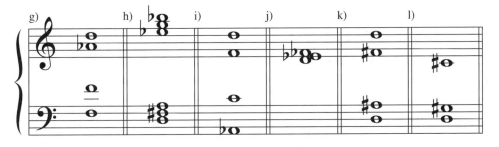

triad, dim   polychord   seventh chord   cluster   triad, aug.   quartal chord

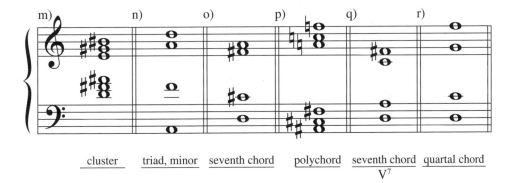

cluster   triad, minor   seventh chord   polychord   seventh chord   quartal chord

V^7

3. See instructions for Exercise 1.

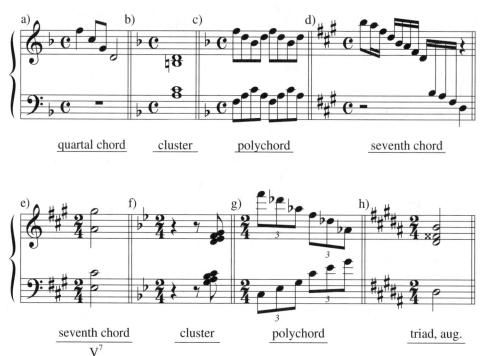

quartal chord   cluster   polychord   seventh chord

seventh chord   cluster   polychord   triad, aug.
V⁷

Opt. EXERCISES (p. 151)

1. Write the following scales in the treble clef, ascending only, using key signatures. Use whole notes. Build a triad on each scale degree. Label the triads with Roman numerals that indicate the qualities of the chords.

a)   D major

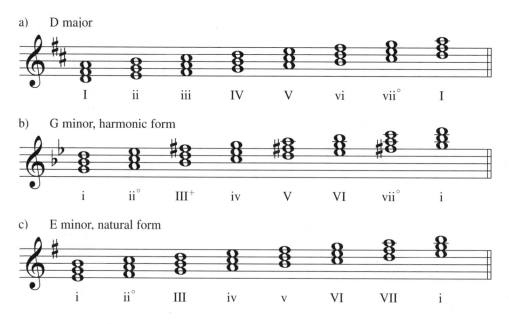

I   ii   iii   IV   V   vi   vii°   I

b)   G minor, harmonic form

i   ii°   III⁺   iv   V   VI   vii°   i

c)   E minor, natural form

i   ii°   III   iv   v   VI   VII   i

2.   Write the popular chord symbol for each of the following.

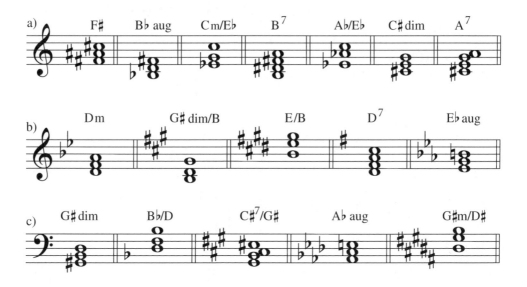

CHAPTER 6

CADENCES AND MELODY WRITING

1 2   **EXERCISES** (p. 155)

1.   Identify the key and the kind of cadence for each of the following.

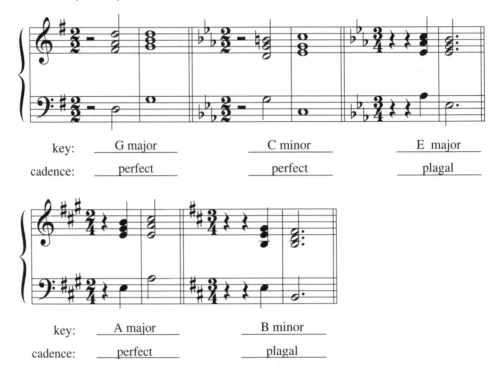

| key: | G major | C minor | E major |
| cadence: | perfect | perfect | plagal |

| key: | A major | B minor |
| cadence: | perfect | plagal |

2.   Write a two-measure example of a perfect cadence in each of the following keys.
Use $\frac{3}{4}$ time. (Sample answers. Other arrangements are possible.)

a) G major   b) D♭ major   c) A major

d) C minor   e) F minor

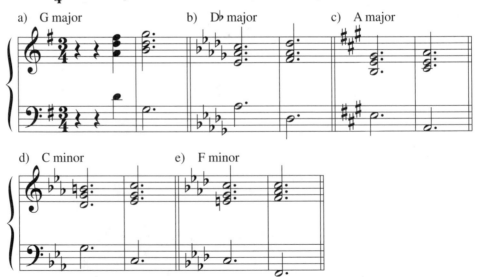

3. Write a two-measure example of a plagal cadence in each of the following keys. Use $\frac{2}{2}$ time. (Sample answers. Other arrangements are possible.)

a) A♭ major   b) B minor   c) F♯ minor

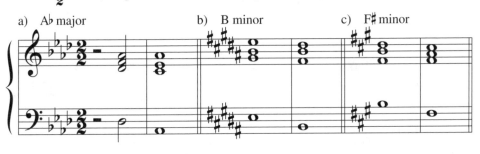

d) E minor   e) E major

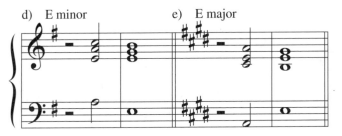

4. The following are melody notes of either perfect or plagal cadences. Complete the cadences and name the type of each. (Sample answers. Other arrangements are possible.)

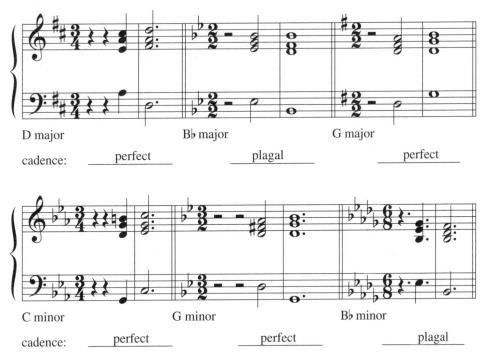

D major cadence: perfect   B♭ major: plagal   G major: perfect

C minor cadence: perfect   G minor: perfect   B♭ minor: plagal

2 EXERCISES (p. 159)

1. For each of the following, name the key, write the Roman numeral for each chord, and name the cadence.

2 2. Write two different examples of imperfect cadences in each of the following keys. Use $\frac{2}{2}$ time. (Sample answers. Other arrangements are possible.)

a) D major

I V IV V

b) B♭ minor

I V IV V

c) G♯ minor

I V IV V

d) A♭ major

I V IV V

e) C minor

I V IV V

f) C# minor

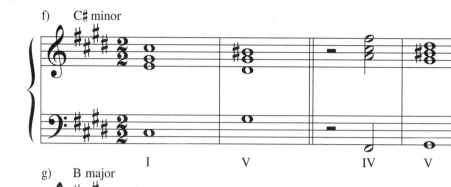

I   V   IV   V

g) B major

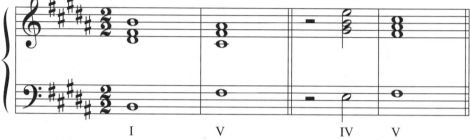

I   V   IV   V

3. Write a two-measure example of each of the three kinds of cadences in each of the
following keys. Use $\frac{3}{2}$ time. (Sample answers. Other arrangements are possible.)

a) A major

V   I   IV   I   IV   V

b) G minor

V   I   IV   I   I   V

c) E minor

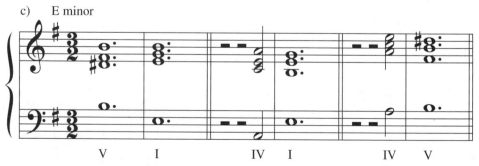

V   I   IV   I   IV   V

4. The following are the melody notes of perfect, plagal, or imperfect cadences. Complete the cadences and name the type of each.

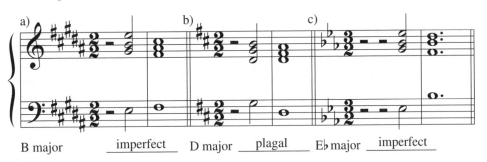

B major ___imperfect___   D major ___plagal___   E♭ major ___imperfect___

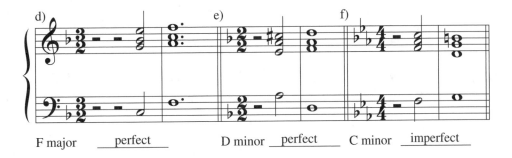

F major ___perfect___   D minor ___perfect___   C minor ___imperfect___

Alternative answers:

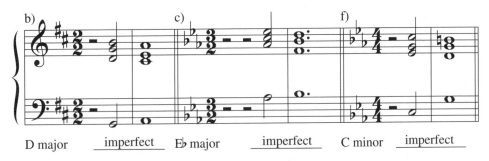

D major ___imperfect___   E♭ major ___imperfect___   C minor ___imperfect___

2 EXERCISES (p. 163)

1. Name the key of each of the following melodies. Write a cadence at the end of each phrase, and name each cadence.

a)

___F♯ minor___   ___imperfect___

106

perfect

b)

C major   imperfect

plagal

c)

B minor   imperfect

perfect

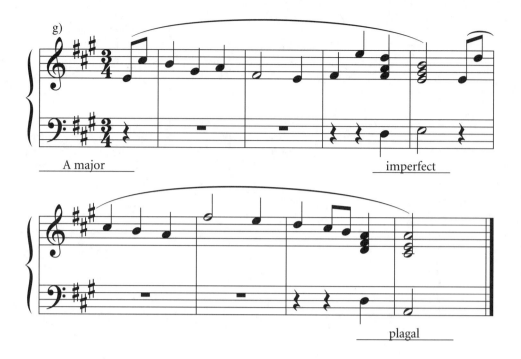

A major

imperfect

plagal

h)

B♭ major

imperfect

perfect

2   EXERCISES (p. 174)

1.   For each of the following:

   • Name the key.
   • Write a cadence at the end of the given phrase and name the cadence.
   • Write an answering phrase for the melody, ending with a perfect cadence.
   • Draw the phrase mark for your answering phrase.

   (Sample answers. Other arrangments are possible.)

a)

key: ___G major___   ___imperfect___

___perfect___

b)

key: ___A major___   ___imperfect___

___perfect___

c)

key: ___A minor___   ___imperfect___

___perfect___

d)

key: ___B♭ major___   ___imperfect___

___perfect___

e)

key: ___B minor___   ___imperfect___

____ perfect

f)

key: ___D minor___ ___imperfect___

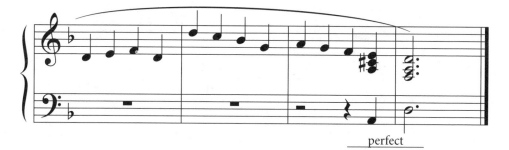

___perfect___

g)

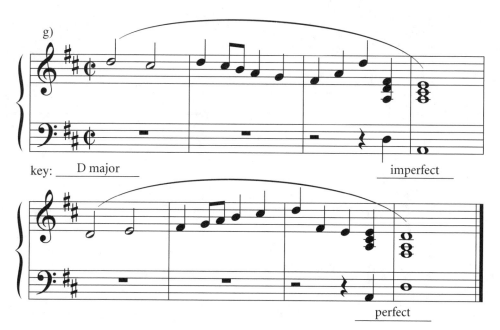

key: ___D major___ ___imperfect___

___perfect___

112

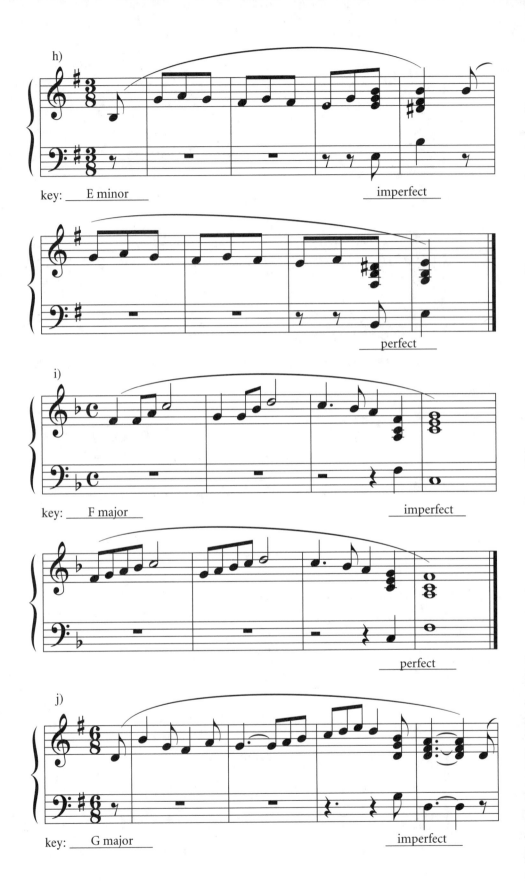

h)

key: ___E minor___   ___imperfect___

___perfect___

i)

key: ___F major___   ___imperfect___

___perfect___

j)

key: ___G major___   ___imperfect___

_____perfect_____

k)

key: ___C minor___   ___imperfect___

_____perfect_____

CHAPTER 7

TIME

P 1 2   EXERCISES (p. 183)

1.   Write two measures, each using a different rhythm, for each of the following time signatures. (Sample answers. Other solutions are possible.)

2.   Add bar lines to each of the following according to the given time signature.

a)

b)

c)

3. Add the correct time signature to each of the following rhythms.

4. Add bar lines to each of the following according to the given time signature.

a)

b)

c)

d)

5. Complete the following measures with rests in the places indicated by the brackets.

6. Add stems to the following and group them correctly to make one complete measure in each of the following time signatures. (Sample answers. Other groupings are possible.)

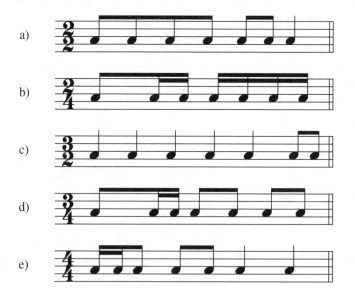

7. Add the correct time signature to each of the following measures.

1 2   EXERCISES (p. 193)

1.   Complete the following measures with rests in the places indicated by the brackets.

2.   Add the correct time signature to each of the following measures.

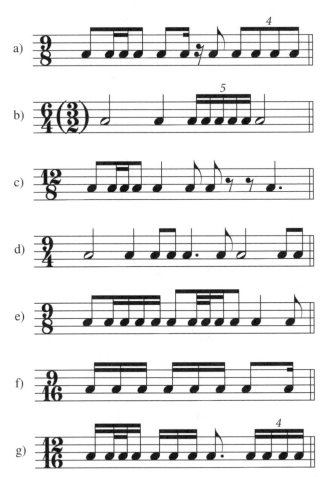

3.   Add bar lines to each of the following according to the given time signatures.

d)

e)

f)

g)

h)

i)

4. Add stems to the following, and group them correctly to make *one* complete measure in each of the following time signatures. (Sample answers. Other groupings are possible.)

a)

b)

c)

d)

5. Re-group the following in $\frac{6}{8}$ time.

6. Re-group the following in $\frac{3}{4}$ time.

7. a) What is the difference between $\frac{6}{8}$ time and $\frac{3}{4}$ time?

b) Write one measure of each, grouping the notes correctly.

a) The difference is: $\frac{6}{8}$ time has 2 groups of 3 eighths per measure,

$\frac{3}{4}$ time has 3 groups of 2 eighths per measure.

b)

8. Write three measures, each using a different rhythm, in each of the following time signatures. You may use dotted notes but not rests. (Sample answers. Other arrangements are possible.)

9.   Complete the following measures with rests.

a)

10.   Complete the following measures with rests.

a)

2   EXERCISES (p. 203)

1.   Complete the following measures with notes showing the two different ways of grouping duple meters.

Example:

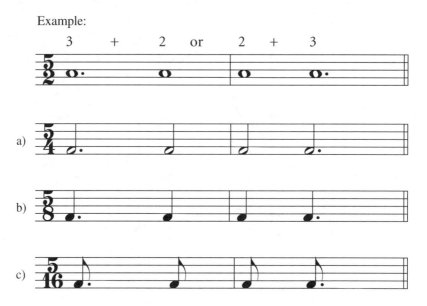

2.   Complete the following measures with notes showing the five different ways of grouping hybrid triple meters.

Example:

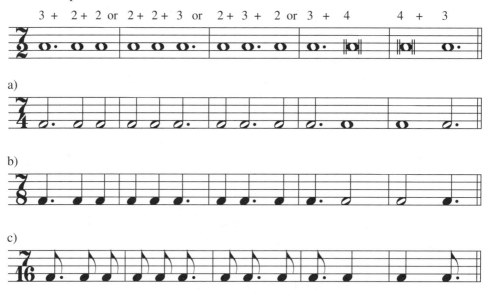

3. Add a time signature to each of the following, and indicate the grouping of the pulses into beats.

Example:

128

4. Complete the following measures with rests in the places indicated by the brackets. (Sample answers. Other groupings are possible.)

CHAPTER 8

NAMING THE KEY, TRANSPOSITION, AND DETECTING ERRORS

P 1 2   EXERCISES (p. 208)

1.   Name the key of each of the following melodies.

a)

key:____C minor_____

b)

key:____E minor_____

c)

key:____G major_____

d)

key:____F# minor_____

130

e)

key: D minor

f)

key: F minor

g)

key: E minor

h)

key: A major

i)

key: G minor

1 2   MORE EXERCISES (p. 210)

1.   Name the key of each of the following melodies.

a)

key:____F major____

b)

key:____B minor____

c)

key:____G major____

P 1 2   EXERCISES (p. 214)

1.   Name the key of the following melody. Transpose it down an octave in the treble clef.

key:____G major____

2. Name the key of the following melody. Transpose it up an octave in the bass clef.

key:____E♭ major____

3. Name the key of the following melody. Transpose it up an octave into the treble clef.

key:____F minor____

4. Name the key of the following melody. Transpose it down an octave into the bass clef.

key:____D major____

5.   Name the key of the following melody. Transpose it down an octave in the treble clef.

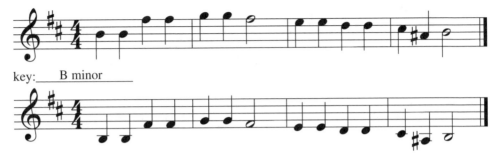

key:_____B minor_____

6.   Name the key of the following melody. Transpose it down an octave into the bass clef.

key:_____D minor_____

7.   Name the key of the following melody. Transpose it up an octave into the treble clef.

key:_____A major_____

8.   Name the key of the following melody. Transpose it down an octave into the bass clef.

key:_____C minor_____

9.   Name the key of the following melody. Transpose it down an octave into the bass clef.

key:____F♯ minor____

10.   Name the key of the following melody. Transpose it down an octave into the bass clef.

key:____F major____

11.   Name the key of the following melody. Transpose it up an octave into the treble clef.

key:____B♭ major____

12. Name the key of the following melody. Transpose it down an octave in the bass clef.

key:___F minor___

13. Name the key of the following melody. Transpose it up an octave into the treble clef.

key:___E major___

14. Name the key of the following melody. Transpose it down an octave in the treble clef.

key:___B♭ major___

15. Name the key of the following melody. Transpose it down an octave into the bass clef.

key:___D major___

1 2   MORE EXERCISES (p. 219)

1. Name the key of the following melody. Rewrite it at the same pitch using the correct key signature and omitting any unnecessary accidentals.

key:___G♭ major___

2.   Name the key of the following melody. Transpose it down an octave into the bass clef.

key:___Eb major___

3.   Name the key of the following melody. Transpose it down an octave into the bass clef.

key:___G major___

4.   Name the key of the following melody. Rewrite it at the same pitch in the treble clef, using the correct key signature and omitting any unnecessary accidentals.

key:___E major___

5.   Name the key of the following melody. Transpose it down an octave into the bass clef, using the correct key signature and omitting any unnecessary accidentals.

key:____F major____

6.   Name the key of the following melody. Transpose it up an octave in the bass clef, using the correct key signature and omitting any unnecessary accidentals.

key:____B major____

7. Name the key of the following melody. Transpose it down an octave into the bass clef, using the correct key signature and omitting any unnecessary accidentals.

key:___Bb major___

2 STILL MORE EXERCISES (p. 222)

1. Name the key of the following melody. Rewrite it at the same pitch in the alto clef, using the correct key signature and omitting any unnecessary accidentals.

key:___E major___

140

2. Name the key of the following melody. Transpose it up an octave into the treble clef.

key:_____D major_____

3. Name the key of the following melody. Rewrite it at the same pitch in the alto clef, using the correct key signature and omitting any unnecessary accidentals.

key:_____C minor_____

4. Name the key of the following melody. Rewrite it an octave lower in the alto clef, using the correct key signature and omitting any unnecessary accidentals.

key:____B major____

1 2   EXERCISES (p. 226)

1. Transpose the following melody into A major.

key:____G major____

2. Transpose the following melody a) into F major b) up a major 3rd. Name the new key.

key:____E♭ major____

a)

b)

key: G major

3. Transpose the following melody a) into G major b) up a perfect 4th. Name the new key.

key: F major

a)

b)

key: B♭ major

4. Transpose the following melody a) up a major 2nd and name the new key b) into A major.

key: E♭ major

a)

key: F major

b)

5.   Transpose the following melody a) up a perfect 4th b) up a major 2nd. In each case, name the new key.

key:___Bb major____

a)

key:___Eb major____

b)

key:___C major____

6.   Transpose the following melody a) up a major 3rd and name the new key
     b) into G major.

key:___F major____

a)

key:___A major____

b)

144

7. Transpose the following melody a) into B♭ major b) into F major.

key:___E major___

a)

b)

8. In what key is the following melody written? Transpose it into D major, using the correct key signature.

key:___B♭ major___

9.   Transpose the following melody a) into A major b) up a major 3rd. Name the new key.

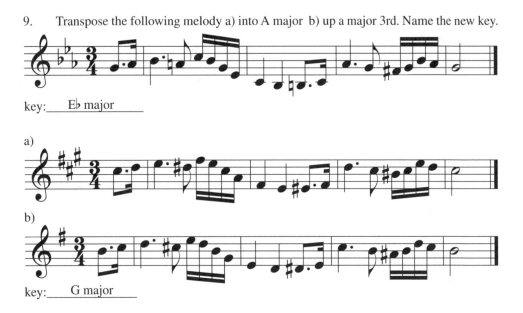

key:____Eb major____

a)

b)

key:____G major____

10.   Transpose the following melody a) into Db major b) up a minor 3rd. Name the new key.

key:____B major____

a)

b)

key:____D major____

2   MORE EXERCISES (p. 231)

1.   Transpose the following melody down a major 2nd. Name the new key.

key:____E minor____

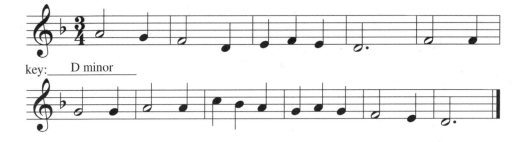

key:___D minor___

2.   Transpose the following melody up a major 2nd. Name the new key.

key:___A minor___

key:___B minor___

3.   Transpose the following melody down a major 2nd. Name the new key.

key:___D minor___

key:___C minor___

4. Transpose the following melody down a major 2nd. Name the new key.

key: ___G minor___

key: ___F minor___

5. Transpose the following melody up a minor 3rd into the alto clef. Name the new key.

key: ___E minor___

key: ___G minor___

6. In what key is the following melody written? Transpose it into G minor, using the correct key signature and omitting any unnecessary accidentals.

key: ___F♯ minor___

7.   In what key is the following melody written? Transpose it down a major 3rd, using the correct key signature and omitting any unnecessary accidentals. Name the new key.

key:____G minor____

key:____E♭ minor____

8.   In what key is the following melody written? Transpose it a) into G minor
     b) into B♭ minor, using the correct key signature and omitting any unnecessary accidentals.

key:____F minor____

a)

b)

9. In what key is the following melody written? Transpose it into E minor, using the correct key signature and omitting any unnecessary accidentals.

key: C minor

10. Transpose the following melody a) into B minor b) up a major 3rd. Name the new key.

key: D minor

a)

b)

key: F# minor

150

11.　In what key is the following melody written? Transpose it a) down a minor 3rd
b) up a minor 2nd, using the correct key signature and omitting any unnecessary
accidentals. In each case, name the new key.

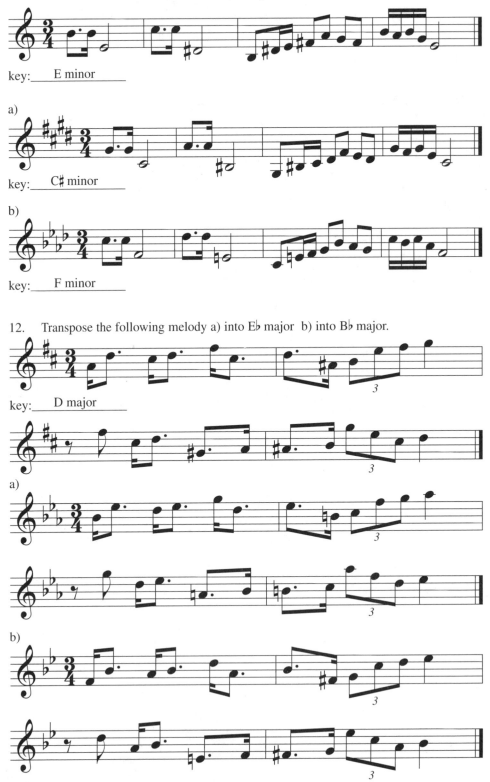

key:＿＿E minor＿＿＿

a)

key:＿＿C♯ minor＿＿＿

b)

key:＿＿F minor＿＿＿

12.　Transpose the following melody a) into E♭ major b) into B♭ major.

key:＿＿D major＿＿＿

a)

b)

2 EXERCISES (p. 238)

1. For each of the following excerpts, name the key in which it is written. Transpose it to concert pitch, using the appropriate new key signature. Name the new key.

a) Trumpet in B♭

The Sleeping Beauty, op. 66, Act I, Valse (No. 6)

key:___C major___

The Sleeping Beauty, op. 66, Act I, Valse (No. 6)

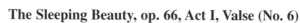

key:___B♭ major___

b) French horn in F

Symphony No. 8, op. 93, 3rd movement

key:___C major___

Symphony No. 8, op. 93, 3rd movement

key:___F major___

c) English horn

Harold in Italy ("Serenade"), op. 16, 3rd movement

key: G major

Harold in Italy ("Serenade"), op. 16, 3rd movement

key: C major

d) Clarinet in B♭

Symphony No. 3, op. 90, 2nd movement

key: D major

Symphony No. 3, op. 90, 2nd movement

key: C major

e)   English horn

Trio, op. 87

L. van Beethoven

key:___G major___

Trio, op. 87

L. van Beethoven

key:___C major___

f)   Clarinet in B♭

Carmen, Acts I–II "Entr'acte"

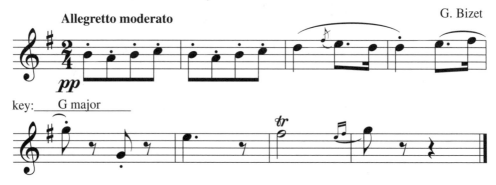

G. Bizet

key:___A major___

Carmen, Acts I–II "Entr'acte"

G. Bizet

key:___G major___

154

g)   English horn

Overture–Fantaisie, Romeo et Juliette

Allegro giusto   P.I. Tchaikovsky

mf *espr.*

key:___Ab major___

Overture–Fantaisie, Romeo et Juliette

Allegro giusto   P.I. Tchaikovsky

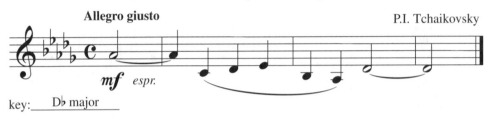

mf *espr.*

key:___Db major___

h)   Clarinet in Bb

A Midsummer Night's Dream, op. 61, "Scherzo"

Allegro vivace   F. Mendelssohn

pp

key:___A minor___

A Midsummer Night's Dream, op. 61, "Scherzo"

Allegro vivace   F. Mendelssohn

pp

key:___G minor___

1 2   **EXERCISES** (p. 242)

1.   Rewrite the following passages of music, correcting the mistakes.

a)

b)

c)

156

d)

dolc

Dolce

e)

moto con

Con moto

2   MORE EXERCISES (p. 244)

1.   Rewrite the following passages of music, correcting the mistakes.

a)

b)

158

CHAPTER 9

SCORE TYPES

2   EXERCISES (p. 250)

1.   Write the following in short (condensed) score.

2.   Write the following passage in open score for string quartet.

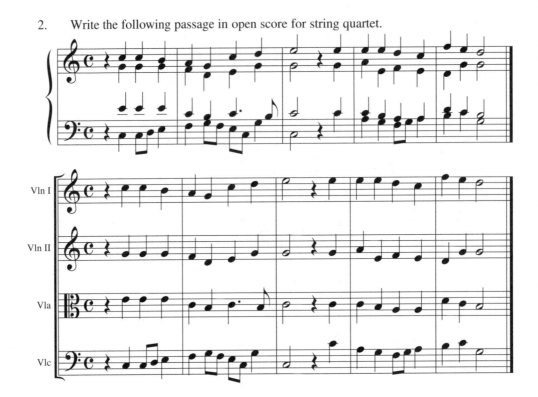

3.   Write the following passage in short (condensed) score.

4   (a) Write the following passage in modern vocal score.

(b) Transpose the above passage into the key of E minor.

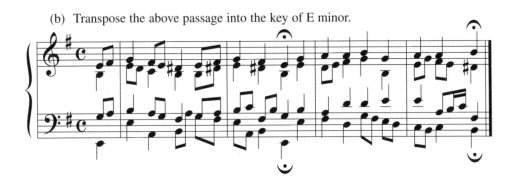

5.   (a) Write the following passage in open score, using C clefs for alto and tenor.

(b) Transpose the above passage up a major 3rd.

6.   (a) Write the following passage in modern vocal score.

(b) Transpose the above passage into A minor.

7. Write the following passage in open score for string quartet.

8. Transpose the following passage down a minor 3rd, writing it in open score, using C clefs for alto and tenor.

CHAPTER 12

ANALYSIS QUESTIONS AND TEST PAPERS

PRELIMINARY ANALYSIS (p. 278)

Analyse the following music excerpt by answering the questions below.

Piano Sonata, Hob. XVI: G1
Finale

F. J. Haydn
(1732–1809)

1. Name the composer of this piece. __F.J. Haydn__

2. Add the correct time signature directly on the music.

3. On which beat does this piece begin? __beat 3__

4. Explain the meaning of *presto*. __very fast__

5. Name the key of this piece. __G major__

6. Find and circle one example of a diatonic semitone. Label it DS. **There are many examples (B to C and F♯ to G).**

7. For the passage at letter **A**:

    a) Name the *harmonic* interval between the notes. __per 8__

    b) Name the technical degree (tonic, supertonic, or dominant) on which this passage begins, and the technical degree on which it ends.

        begins on: __tonic__   ends on: __dominant__

8. Name the interval at letter **B**. __min 3__

9. Explain the sign at letter **C**. __repeat sign – repeat from the beginning__

166

GRADE ONE ANALYSIS (p. 279)

Analyse the following music excerpt by answering the questions below.

Piano Sonata, K 545
2nd movement

W. A. Mozart
(1756–1791)

1. Add the correct time signature directly on the music.

2. Explain the meaning of *andante*. rather slow; at a moderate, walking pace

3. Name the key of this piece. G major

4. Name the triad at letter **A**.

   root: G   position: root position   quality: major

5. Name the triad at letter **B**.

   root: C   position: 2nd inv.   quality: major

6. Name the interval at letter **C**. aug 4

7. Name the interval at letter **D**. min 6

8. Name the triad at letter **E**.

   root: E   position: root position   quality: minor

9. Name the triad at letter **F**.

   root: G   position: 1st inv.   quality: major

10. Name the harmonic interval on beat 2 of m. 8 of the left-hand part.

   maj 3

GRADE TWO ANALYSIS (p. 280)

Analyse the following music excerpt by answering the questions below.

Bagatelle, op. 119, no. 1

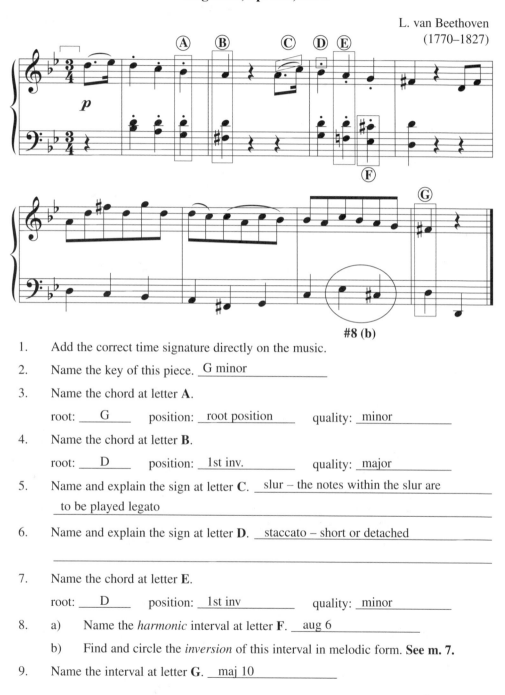

L. van Beethoven
(1770–1827)

#8 (b)

1. Add the correct time signature directly on the music.

2. Name the key of this piece. <u>G minor</u>

3. Name the chord at letter **A**.

    root: <u>G</u>   position: <u>root position</u>   quality: <u>minor</u>

4. Name the chord at letter **B**.

    root: <u>D</u>   position: <u>1st inv.</u>   quality: <u>major</u>

5. Name and explain the sign at letter **C**. <u>slur – the notes within the slur are</u>
    <u>to be played legato</u>

6. Name and explain the sign at letter **D**. <u>staccato – short or detached</u>

7. Name the chord at letter **E**.

    root: <u>D</u>   position: <u>1st inv</u>   quality: <u>minor</u>

8. a)   Name the *harmonic* interval at letter **F**. <u>aug 6</u>

    b)   Find and circle the *inversion* of this interval in melodic form. **See m. 7.**

9. Name the interval at letter **G**. <u>maj 10</u>

Marks **PRELIMINARY TEST PAPER** (p. 281)

(10) 1. a) Write the following as half notes in the bass clef.

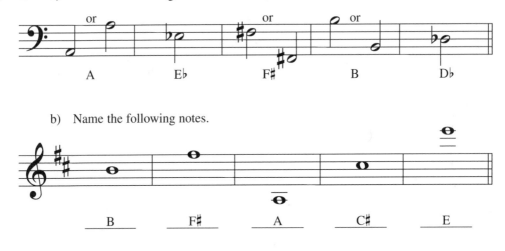

A   Eb   F♯   B   Db

b) Name the following notes.

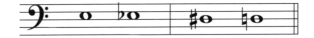

B   F♯   A   C♯   E

(10) 2. a) Write a whole tone above each of the following notes.

b) Write a chromatic semitone below each of the following notes.

(10) 3. Write the following scales, ascending and descending, using whole notes.

a) E major in the treble clef, using accidentals
b) Ab major in the bass clef, using a key signature
c) F♯ minor, natural form, in the bass clef, using a key signature
d) G minor, harmonic form, in the bass clef, using accidentals
e) C minor, melodic form, in the treble clef, using a key signature

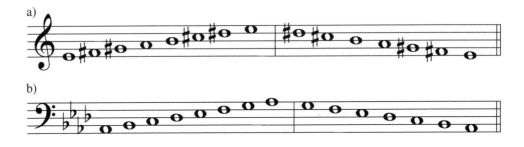

c)

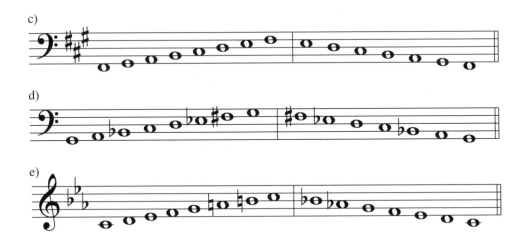

d)

e)

(10) 4. Write the following notes in the bass clef, using accidentals.

     a) the tonic of E minor
     b) the subdominant of F major
     c) the dominant of B minor
     d) the tonic of A♭ major
     e) the dominant of F♯ minor

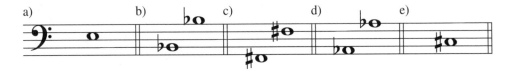

(10) 5. a) Write the following intervals above the given notes.

per 4   maj 7   min 6   per 5   maj 2

     b) Name the following intervals.

min 3   per 8   maj 6   min 2   maj 3

(10) 6.   Write the following triads in the treble clef, using key signatures.

      a) the subdominant triad of A major
      b) the dominant triad of C♯ minor harmonic
      c) the tonic triad of B♭ major
      d) the dominant triad of E♭ major
      e) the subdominant triad of D minor harmonic

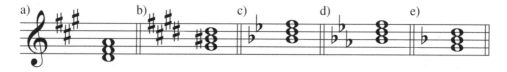

(10) 7.   Add rests below the brackets to complete the following measures.

(10) 8.   a)   Name the key of the following melody. Transpose it down one octave into the
          bass clef.

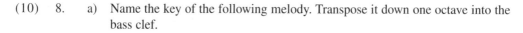

key:_____G minor_____

b) Name the key of the following melody. Transpose it up one octave into the treble clef.

key:____D major_____

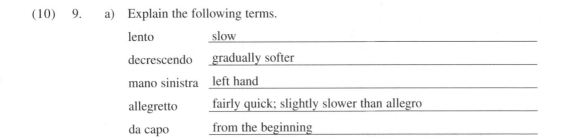

(10)　9.　a)　Explain the following terms.

　　　　　　lento　　　　　　　slow_____

　　　　　　decrescendo　　gradually softer_____

　　　　　　mano sinistra　left hand_____

　　　　　　allegretto　　　fairly quick; slightly slower than allegro_____

　　　　　　da capo　　　　from the beginning_____

　　　　b)　Draw the following signs on the given notes.

　　　　　tie　　　　　　　fermata　　　　staccato　　　　　slur　　　　　accent

(10)　10.　a)　Analyse the following melody by answering the questions below:

　　　　　　・ Name its key.
　　　　　　・ Add the correct time signature.
　　　　　　・ Circle and label the subdominant note.
　　　　　　・ Circle and label the tonic triad.
　　　　　　・ Circle and label the dominant triad.

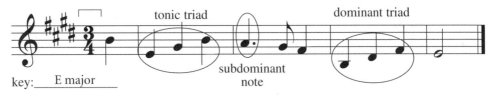

key:____E major_____

b) Analyse the following melody by answering the questions below:

- Name its key.
- Add the correct time signature.
- Circle and label the dominant note. (There are three examples.)
- Circle and label a diatonic semitone. (There are five examples.)
- Circle and label an interval of a minor 6th.

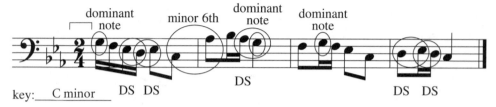

key: C minor

Marks   **GRADE ONE TEST PAPER** (p. 286)

(10)   1.   a)   Write the following scales, ascending and descending, using the correct key signature for each. Use whole notes.

Cb major in the treble clef

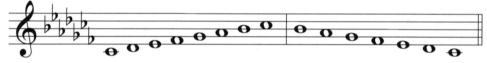

D# minor, melodic form, in the bass clef

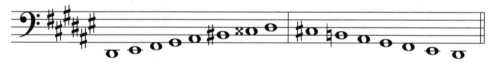

chromatic scale on Bb in the treble clef

b)   Identify the following scale types.

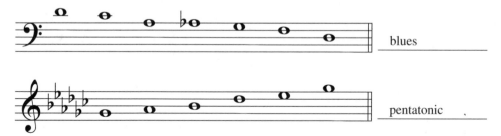

blues

pentatonic

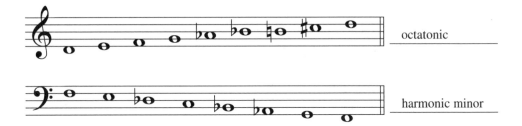

octatonic

harmonic minor

(10) 2. Write the following notes in the bass clef, using accidentals.

   a) the supertonic of A♭ major
   b) the leading note of G♯ minor harmonic
   c) the subdominant of F minor
   d) the submediant of B major
   e) the mediant of C minor

(10) 3. a) Write the following intervals above the given notes.

perf 4   aug 6   min 3   maj 7   dim 5

   b) Invert the above intervals and name the inversions.

per 5   dim 3   maj 6   min 2   aug 4

(10) 4. Write the following triads in the treble clef, using key signatures.

   a) the supertonic triad of A major in root position
   b) the dominant triad of B♭ minor harmonic in first inversion
   c) the submediant triad of E♭ major in root position
   d) the tonic triad of C♯ minor in second inversion
   e) the subdominant triad of G minor harmonic in first inversion

174

(10) 5. Write a two-measure example of each of the following cadences.

      a) perfect cadence in E major
      b) plagal cadence in D minor
      c) perfect cadence in B minor
      (Sample answers. Other arrangements are possible.)

(10) 6. Add rests below the brackets to complete the following measures. (Sample answers. Alternatives are possible.)

(10) 7. For each of the following melodies, name the key and add the correct time signature.

key: ___E major___

key: ___B♭ major___

key:___C minor___

key:___E minor___

key:___F minor___

(10) 8. a) Name the key of the following melody. Transpose it up an augmented 4th using the correct new key signature. Name the new key.

key:___D♭ major___

key:___G major___

b) Name the key of the following melody. Transpose it up a minor 3rd using the correct new key signature. Name the new key.

key:___F major___

key:___A♭ major___

(10) 9. a) Explain the following terms.

fortepiano   loud, then immediately soft

vivace   quick and lively

leggiero   light

grave   extremely slow and solemn

accelerando   gradually getting quicker

b) Give the Italian word or phrase for each of the following.

but   ma

with   con

little by little   poco a poco

more   più

not too much   non troppo

(10) 10. Analyse the following music excerpt by answering the questions below.

Kinder-Sonate, op. 118a, no. 1
1st movement

R. Schumann
(1810–1856)

a) Name the composer of this piece. ___R. Schumann___

b) Name the key of this piece. ___G major___

c) How many times is the mediant note played in this piece? ___16 times___
   ___(17 if the unison in m. 3 is counted as 2)___

d) Explain the two signs at letter **A**. ___crescendo – becoming louder;___
   ___decrescendo – becoming softer___

e) Explain the sign at letter **B**. ___fortepiano – loud, then suddenly soft___
   _____

f) Name the interval at letter **C**. ___min 7___

g) Name the interval at letter **D**. ___per 1___

h) Name the triad at letter **E**.
   root: ___D___   position: ___root position___   quality: ___major___

i) Name the triad at letter **F**.
   root: ___C___   position: ___1st inv.___   quality: ___major___

j) Name the triad at letter **G**.
   root: ___G___   position: ___2nd inv.___   quality: ___major___

Marks   **GRADE TWO TEST PAPER** (p. 291)

(10) 1.   a) Write the following scales and mode, ascending and descending, using the
             correct key signature for each. Use whole notes.

C♯ major, from supertonic to supertonic, in the tenor clef

E♭ minor, harmonic form, from dominant to dominant, in the bass clef

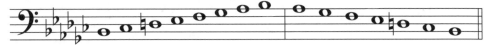

Dorian mode on B♭ in the treble clef

b) Write the following scale and mode, ascending and descending, using accidentals. Use whole notes.

G♯ minor, melodic form, from subdominant to subdominant, in the alto clef

Lydian mode on E in the bass clef

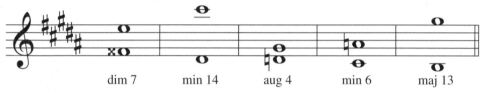

(10) 2.   a)   Write the following intervals below the given notes.

dim 7   min 14   aug 4   min 6   maj 13

b) Invert the above intervals in the bass clef, and name the inversions.

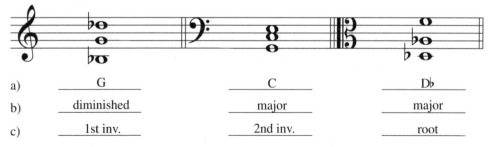

aug 2   maj 2   dim 5   maj 3   min 3

(10) 3.   For each of the following triads, name:
a) its root
b) its position
c) its quality

a)	G	C	D♭
b)	diminished	major	major
c)	1st inv.	2nd inv.	root

d) Name the scale that contains all of these triads. F minor, harmonic form

(10) 4. Write the following dominant 7th chords in the bass clef, using key signatures.

  a) the dominant 7th of A major in second inversion
  b) the dominant 7th of C minor in first inversion
  c) the dominant 7th of B major in third inversion
  d) the dominant 7th of D♯ minor in root position
  e) the dominant 7th of G minor in third inversion

(10) 5. For the following:
  a) Name the key.
  b) Write a cadence at the end of the first phrase, and name the cadence.
  c) Write an answering phrase for the melody, ending with a perfect cadence.
      Draw the phrase mark for your answering phrase.

key: F♯ minor

imperfect

(10) 6. a) Add rests below the brackets to complete the following measures.
      (Sample answers. Some alternatives are possible.)

b) Add the correct time signature to each of the following.

(10) 7. a) Name the key of the following melody. Transpose it up an augmented 6th in the same clef, using the correct new key signature. Name the new key.

key:___Ab major___

key:___F# major___

b) The following melody is written for clarinet in Bb. Name the key in which it is written. Transpose it to concert pitch, using the correct new key signature. Name the new key.

key:___G major___

key:___F major___

(10) 8. a) Rewrite the following passage in modern vocal score. Name the voice that sings each line.

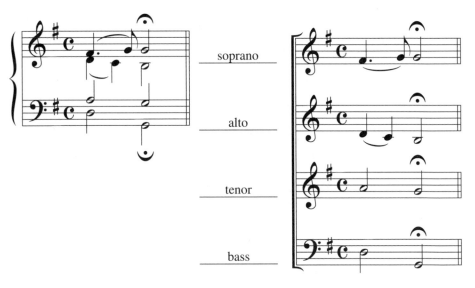

____ soprano ____

____ alto ____

____ tenor ____

____ bass ____

b) The following passage is for string quartet. Name the instrument that plays each line. Rewrite the passage in short score.

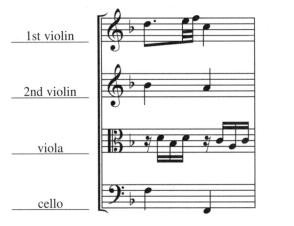

____ 1st violin ____

____ 2nd violin ____

____ viola ____

____ cello ____

182

(10) 9.   a)   Give an Italian term that has the same meaning as each of the following.

léger   leggiero

vite   allegro

langsam   lento

mässig   moderato

mit Ausdruck   con espressione

b)   Define each of the following.

triad   a chord consisting of a root, a 3rd, and a 5th

7th chord   a chord consisting of a root, a 3rd, a 5th, and a 7th

quartal chord   a chord built on a series of fourths

polychord   a combination of two or more different chords

cluster   a chord consisting of at least three adjacent notes of a scale

(10) 10. Analyse the following music excerpt by answering the questions below.

Kinder-Sonate, op. 118a, no. 1
2nd movement

R. Schumann
(1810–1856)

a) In what year was the composer of this piece born? __1810__

b) Name the key of this piece. __E minor__

c) Add the correct time signature directly on the music.

d) Name the interval at letter **A**. __min 6__

e) Name the interval at letter **B**. __maj 10__

f) Name the chord at letter **C**.

   root: __B__   position: __3rd inv.__   quality: __V⁷__

g) Name the chord at letter **D**.

   root: __F♯__   position: __1st inv.__   quality: __diminished__

h) Name the chord at letter **E**.

   root: __E__   position: __2nd inv.__   quality: __minor__

i) Name the the type of cadence at the end of this excerpt. __perfect__

j) Explain the meaning of *langsam*. __slow__